MW00443202

A Simpler Guide to Gmail

An unofficial user guide to setting up and using Gmail, Inbox and Google Calendar

Ceri Clark

A Simpler Guide to Gmail: An unofficial user guide to setting up and using Gmail, Inbox and Google Calendar

Fourth Edition

Copyright © 2018 Ceri Clark

Published by
Lycan Books
Apt 12199, Chynoweth House
Trevissome Park
Truro
TR4 8UN

Phone: 0845 869 2802

ISBN-10: 1909236136

ISBN-13: 978-1909236134

In association with Myrddin Publishing

All rights reserved. No part of this publication may be reproduced, stored in or introduced into a retrieval system, or transmitted, in any form, or by any means (electronic, mechanical, photocopying, recording or otherwise) without the prior written permission of the author. Any person who does any unauthorized act in relation to this publication may be liable to criminal prosecution and civil claims for damages.

Limited Liability/Disclaimer of Warranty: While best efforts have been used in preparing this book, the author and publisher make no representations or warranties of any kind and assume no liabilities of any kind with respect to the accuracy or completeness of the contents and specifically disclaim any implied warranties of merchantability or fitness of use for a particular purpose. Neither the author nor the publisher shall be held liable or responsible to any person or entity with respect to any loss or incidental or consequential damages caused, or alleged to have been caused, directly or indirectly without limitations, by the information or programs contained herein. Furthermore readers should be aware that internet sites listed in this work may have changed or disappeared from when this work was written to when it will be read. This work is sold with the understanding that the advice given herein may not be suitable for every situation.

Trademarks: Where trademarks are used in this book this infers no endorsement or any other affiliation with this book. Any trademarks used in this book are solely used for editorial purposes.

© 2018 Cover & Interior Design: Lycan Books

Photo element © Deposit Photos / brickrena

Contents

06 Your Contacts

Learn how to get to Google Contacts, get an overview of the website, how to add, edit, delete contacts, (and then restore them again), star your contacts and group them using labels.

Find out how to import and export your contacts as well as printing your contacts list. What are *Other Contacts* and where to find them and finally, get to grips with the settings at the end of the chapter.

07 Email Organization with Labels

Organize your email with labels. Discover how to apply, create, customize, edit and remove them.

08 Filters and Blocked Addresses

Automate your organization by creating and editing filters. Learn how to delete them but also share them with friends. Block email addresses to stop receiving unwanted email.

09 Searching for, and in Emails

Uncover Google's advanced search capabilities within Gmail itself. Search in your labels, from certain people, sent emails, using the email subject, keywords (Has the words...). and by removing emails from the search.

Find emails with an attachment and search through your chat conversations. This chapter also covers searching by size, by date, and sorting emails by newest or oldest.

10 Changing the Look and Feel

Change how your Gmail homepage will look with display density and themes.

11 Under the Hood - Gmail Settings

Discover what settings are available under the General, Labels, Inbox, Accounts and import, Filters and blocked addresses, Forwarding and POP/IMAP, Add-ons, Chat, Labs, Offline, and Themes tabs.

18 Gmail Labs

Turbo-charge your Gmail experience with Gmail labs. The labs covered are: Auto-advance, Canned responses, Custom keyboard shortcuts, Google Calendar gadget, Mark as read button, Multiple inboxes, Preview pane, Right-side chat and Smartlabels.

20 Google Calendar

Google Calendar integrates with Gmail. In this chapter find a Calendar overview, how to get there and see how multiple calendars can organize your life,

Learn how to add, configure, create, delete, edit, export, import, share and view calendars. Color-code your calendars to find events quickly, Change the appearance and view of your calendars to make you work more effectively.

Find out how to create, delete (and get them back), and respond to events.

Discover flairs, how to find and use the settings available and even embed your calendar into your website. Find out how to print your calendar, set goals and create reminders and tasks. Finally, see what keyboard shortcuts can be used with Google Calendar.

19 Frequently Asked Questions

I have had many questions over the years, and this chapter aims to cover them, these include; where to go to login to Gmail, what to do if you lose your password, how to change your password, is a particular browser required to use Gmail, how to print email, how to remove the 'extra' inboxes like updates, social and promotions, how to remove email addresses when replying to all, increasing the size of the text in browsers and adding images to emails.

Dedication

My special thanks go to my husband whose swift editing made this book possible.

May I ask for a favor?

Hello, my name is Ceri and I love creating useful and fun books. May I ask for a review at your favorite online retailer if you found this book useful? You will have my undying gratitude and you might help someone else take the plunge and give this book a try. Thank you so much for buying this, I hope you enjoy it as much as I did making it!

Introduction

Dear reader, thank you for choosing A Simpler Guide to Gmail. With over a billion users, Gmail is the most popular email service available. This book is all about how you can get the most out of Google's answer to email, the instant online way to communicate over the internet. It is written to help new users learn the basics and discover features that are far and above better than the closest competition. This book assumes the reader knows the basics of using a computer and has used a browser.

How should I use this book?

If you have never used Gmail before then the first few chapters explain how to set up your account, how to keep your account secure and the basics of sending and receiving email. Following this there are tips on using the excellent tools that will make organizing your email a breeze for the more experienced users. If this is you, the book is designed so that you can dip in at your level. The contents page will give you an overview of what is in the book thematically but if you want to find something specific, the index at the back is a good place to look.

For the purposes of this guide I have made a few assumptions. The first is that you have (or at least have access to) a computer, you are familiar with using a mouse and know what the internet is.

A small disclaimer at this point. Gmail is constantly evolving and while this book is as accurate as could be made possible at the time of publication, Gmail can and will change. Features will be added and others taken away, however the principles will remain the same.

In the e-book version of this book, the images may appear

Did you know...

Gmail has over a billion users while Outlook (Hotmail) has over 400 million.

smaller due to restrictions laid down by retailer and/or download costs. I have tried to write the book in such a way that the images illustrate a point rather than show you how to do a task. For example I will tell you where on the screen a button is and the image will be there as a visual clue but you should be able to find it from the written instructions.

If you have bought this book as a Kindle book, I recommend downloading the Kindle for PC/Mac programs from Amazon (free) to view the book from your computer. You will be able to click on links and the images will be of better quality.

What is Gmail?

Gmail is Google's answer for providing free online email. Email is a way of communicating via text and images sent over the internet. It is the cheapest way of contacting someone, no stamps or per-minute call charges.

There are a myriad of other email solutions on the internet, some of them are free, others charge and a few are a combination of the two. Google likes to do things differently and they've improved how I deal with my correspondence. With the use of labels, filters, contacts and even labs, you will find that Gmail can almost be your own personal secretary, and best of all, it is free!

Why Gmail?

In my opinion, Google offers the best service for email because:

- Easy to use
- Nothing to install
- Over 15 gigabytes of space (enough for a lifetime of email, although this total is/can be shared between other Google services)
- Spell Checking
- Address Book (Contacts)

- Mobile and desktop access (there are apps for your iPhone or Android mobile phones, although any phone capable of using a browser can use it)
- Gmail has possibly the best spam (unwanted email) protection in the world!
- Your username and password for Gmail works for all the other free Google services like Search, YouTube, Chrome and Google+ etc.
- The integration between other services means that if an attachment is too large to send, you can upload it to your Google Drive account and send a link through your email. This effectively means that if you change a document after you have sent your link, then your colleague or friend will get the latest version of whatever you are working on whether it is a business proposal or a wedding invitation list.
- So what are you waiting for, open an account today!

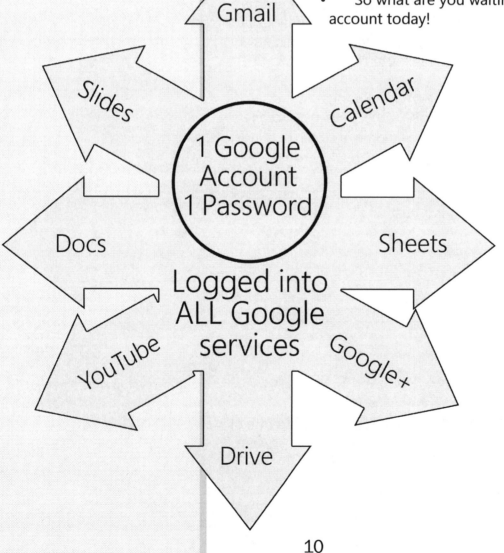

Chapter 01

Opening an Account

What to expect in this chapter:

- Where to go to join Gmail

- Filling in the form

- Choosing passwords

First you need to create your Gmail account. Head over to the account set up page. At the top of your browser, (in your address bar, labelled (**A**) below) type in **gmail.com** or **mail.google.com**. Google will immediately change this and redirect you to the current URL they are using as their homepage (this does change over time). *Figure 1.1* shows what this looks like in the Microsoft Edge browser. Once the new page loads, please click on **Create an account (B)** as also shown in *Figure 1.1*.

You will then be taken to the page as illustrated in *Figure 1.2* to open a Google Account:

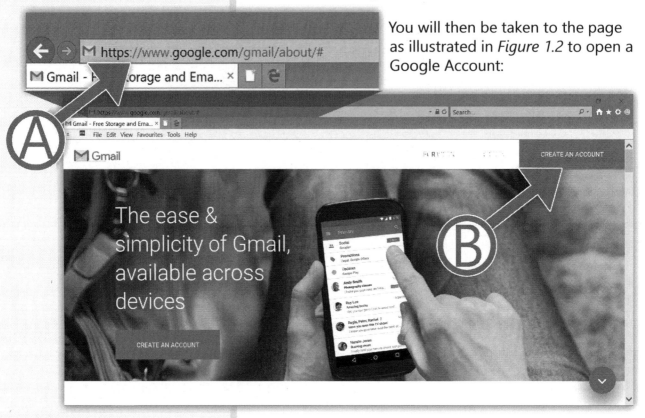

FIGURE 1.1 Creating your account.

Filling in the form

Please make sure you fill in all the boxes you can in the form. Your mobile number is requested for security reasons. If you cannot get into your account for any reason in the future, Google can send you a text message so you can get back in. The same with your email address. If the one you are creating will be your only email address, don't worry, you will still be able to get into your account.

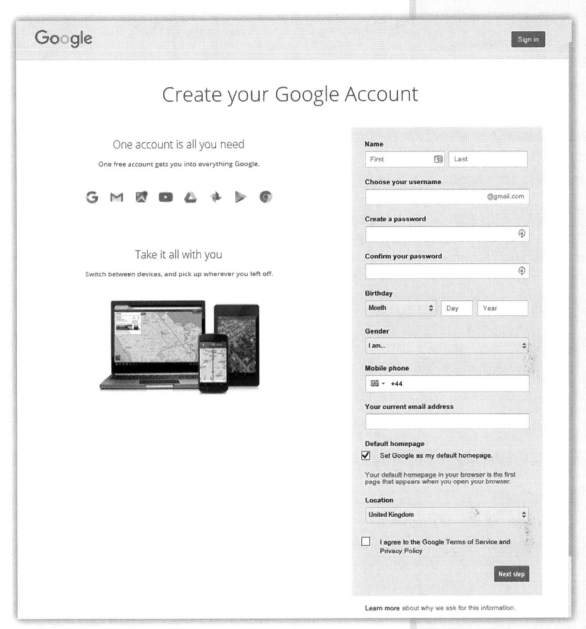

FIGURE 1.2 Sign-in form.

Choosing your username

Your username will be your new email address.
I recommend choosing something that won't
be embarrassing later. You may apply for jobs
or be using this email address in your business.
Fluffywuffychocolateguzzler may sound funny and may
even be free when you type it in but future employers or
business contacts may not be so impressed.

The idea is to create an address of the form
<username>@gmail.com where you are picking the

Did you know...

Opening a Google account doesn't just give you email, by creating this account you can use all Google services with one username and password.

<username> bit before the @ symbol. You can use letters, numbers and periods (full stops).

When you put in your desired username, Google will automatically check to see if it is available, if not, the following (*figure 1.3*) will appear.

Notice how Google gives you a few pointers below your choices for some names that are available. You can choose one of those but being a bit more creative can look more appropriate (read professional) than putting a number on the end. For example, if you have put in your abbreviated first name, then your full first name may be more suitable or even putting in your middle name.

Type in different variants or choose one of their suggestions until you find one that you like and is available.

Choosing your password

Next Google will ask you to choose a password. The most important thing to remember is to make it as strong as possible. Alone, passwords can be hacked. Together with two-factor authentication, they are a powerful preventative and will scupper many a would-be opportunist hacker.

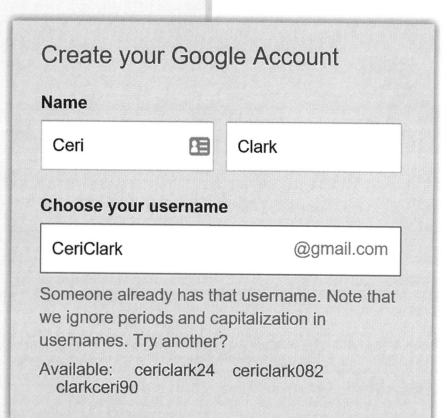

Create your Google Account

Name

Ceri	Clark

Choose your username

CeriClark	@gmail.com

Someone already has that username. Note that we ignore periods and capitalization in usernames. Try another?

Available: cericlark24   cericlark082   clarkceri90

FIGURE 1.3 Username not available.

Whenever possible passwords should only be *part* of your strategy for keeping your Google account safe. If possible always use 2-factor authentication as well. Please see *Chapter 4 Security* or *A Simpler Guide to Online Security* for more information.

Your password needs to be strong. There are a few schools of thought when it comes to thinking up passwords, so here I am going to cover five ways. Whatever you choose, there should be a minimum of 8 characters in your password. If possible, these should be a mixture of lower and upper-case letters, numbers and special characters such as a $, *, &, @ and punctuation etc.

Option 1:

The simplest one to remember is choosing three random words, which mean something to you but would be impossible to guess for an outsider. For example, if your favorite food is cake, your favorite vacation was in Hawaii and you just love baseball, then as much as my spell check hates it, cakeHawaiibaseball could be considered a reasonable password.

Option 2:

Another way to choose a password is by using a combination of letters, numbers and special characters. Using everyday words can make it easy to remember. For example, Elephantsrock is bad, but El3ph@nt5r0ck is strong. To get El3ph@nt5r0ck, I replaced an e with a three, the a with @ symbol, s with five and o with zero. All the replacement numbers look like their letter counterparts to make it easy to remember.

Option 3:

The third way is to choose a phrase, which you will remember and take the first letters of each word, for example: "The scariest movie I have seen is Omen!" Once you have settled on a phrase just add a special character and number. I saw the film when I was about 9 so that's the number I will choose here. The password in this example would be: TsmihsiO!9

Option 4:

Another way to choose a password is similar to the above method but involves an aid. Those familiar with the 2011 movie *Unknown* starring Liam Neeson may recognize this method. If you have a favorite book then choose a passage and from that passage choose a word. For example, if the word is in the 22nd line on page 150, two words along and the word is mammoth, the word would be 150222mammoth, or any combination of these elements that is easy for you to remember.

Option 5:

Another method to create a highly secure password is to create a spreadsheet on your computer or write them in password books and record all your passwords. The secret here is that you only type half of the password in your file. What you record in the book or database needs to be random with a combination of characters. The reason that this method is secure is that half of the password is *only stored in your head*. It does not matter where you put the memorised half of the password into the complete password (at the beginning, middle or end) as long as it is not written down. An example could be:

Memorised half (only in your head): wind

Recorded half (in book, spreadsheet or database): Hydf54j@#f

For this half you could use a password generator or mash the keyboard. It really doesn't matter as long as it is random.

Full password while logging in: windHydf54j@#f

As you can see this method would make your passwords difficult to guess. You should not store it in a password vault service unless you put it behind something protected by 2-step authentication.

If you are like me and are liable to forget passwords, a good way to cheat is to use a service such as LastPass. Sign

Tip...

Example

Memorized half (only in your head):

wind

Recorded half (in a book or databse):

Hydf54j@#f

Full password while logging in:

windHydf54j@#f

up at **lastpass.com** and use their service to either generate passwords for you or to remember passwords you have made. You will need one password to use LastPass but the service will remember all your other login information and can automatically log you in to websites. The service is free and will also work on your mobile devices.

This way you can have different passwords for all the websites you visit and only have to remember the one to get into LastPass which stores all the impossible to remember ones. The service will also warn you when websites have been known to be compromised and ask you to change your password for them. If you have used a different password (auto-generated) for each website you will only need to change the one password. I highly recommend having a different password for each site so that if a hacker manages to get to a shopping site and steals your password associated with you username or email then they won't be able to use that password for your bank or any other site.

I would like to say a word of warning though. If you use this service make sure that you set up the password recovery options. You will need to install the LastPass plugin and have setup the recovery information. The service is very secure and if you have not done this and you have lost or forgotten your password, then there is no way of getting back the contents of your password database. You can generate a one-time password for emergencies.

To be very secure with LastPass, set up two-factor authentication. This means that you will need both a password and your phone (or other physical device) to be able to login. A hacker will not usually have access to your phone and if they do steal it, you will still be protected by the password. If your phone was stolen, you would then automatically change your password and use the recovery information to regain access to Lastpass.

Let's get back to making our account.

Did you know...

Use option 5 with password keepers or online password managers to help keep your passwords safe.

For a large selection of password keepers disguised to look like an ordinary book you can hide in plain sight on your bookshelf, take a look at:

https://passwordkeeperbooks.com

Birthday, gender, mobile phone and email address

The first two elements in this section are self-explanatory, although if you are sensitive about your birthday, I have known people to put a different birthday in here. Just remember what you entered!

Your mobile phone will be used to text a code to you to prove who you are when resetting your account in circumstances where you have forgotten your password. You will also be contacted by your email address if you have a separate one. It is recommended that you give Google an accurate mobile phone and email address when you sign up. You need a way in if you forget your password.

Default homepage

Click this check box if you want Google to be the first thing you see when you open your browser. This is handy if the first thing you do each day is check your email. There is a link at the top right of the screen that will take you straight to your inbox.

Location

Choose the country where you currently reside. This will make sure that your emails have the correct date and time for where you are. If the wrong location is set it could look like you are time travelling in the past to send emails (the time difference between the UK and USA for example). Another reason to choose the right location is to make sure you have the right terms and conditions for your country.

Terms of service

Make sure you read the Google Terms of Service. You will not be able to open an

FIGURE 1.4 Verification.

18

account unless you accept them.

Click on **Next step.**

You will be asked to verify your
account. Type in your phone
number and choose whether
you want Google to send you a
verification code by text message
or through a phone call. Click on
Continue.

FIGURE 1.5 You will be asked to
verify your account.

Check your phone or wait for the phone call from Google.
Once you have the verification number add it to the screen
that loaded when you clicked on Continue.

Click on **Continue** again and a welcome screen will load.

Google's welcome screen will prompt you to setup/update
your profile (upper right) or go straight to **Continue to
Gmail** (blue button). You can go straight to Gmail and fill
in your profile information later. In fact, you do not need
to fill in your profile information at all if you do not want
to. If you do, your contacts will be able to see who you are
from their address books. It is nice to see a little picture
of your friends or contacts when you open an email. It
reassures them/you that the email is from that person and
not someone spoofing their email, which happens. A word
of warning, just because an email says it is from someone

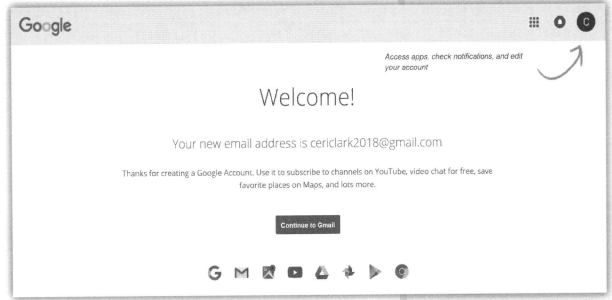

FIGURE 1.6 Welcome to
your new email account

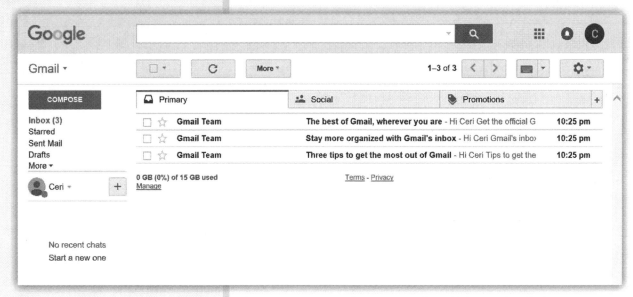

FIGURE 1.7 First look at your new account.

doesn't necessarily mean it is. Click on the little arrow next to your name for a quick check for more information to see exactly from where the email was sent from.

If you continue on to Gmail, you will be given a quick overview of what Gmail can do. Click on **Go to Gmail** at the end of this.

You can also go to the top and click on the letter (the first initial of your name) to change your profile/account details. I will be explaining how to set up your account later in this book.

Here's is how your inbox will look when you first sign up:

Chapter summary

Google has made it easy to set up a Gmail account. This chapter discussed how to choose a username and password and why Google asks for certain information. Security is important on the internet and if you can choose a secure password and set up your account so that Google can notify you of any suspicious use of your account then you will go a long way to protecting your information and privacy. *Chapter 4 Security* will go into more detail on how you can secure your account even more.

Chapter 02

An Overview

What to expect in this chapter:

- An introduction to the top and dropdown navigation bars

- An overview of the options available from the homepage

An overview

The Gmail homepage can look a little intimidating when you first look at it. This chapter aims to give you a brief explanation of the main elements on the page to give you a head start.

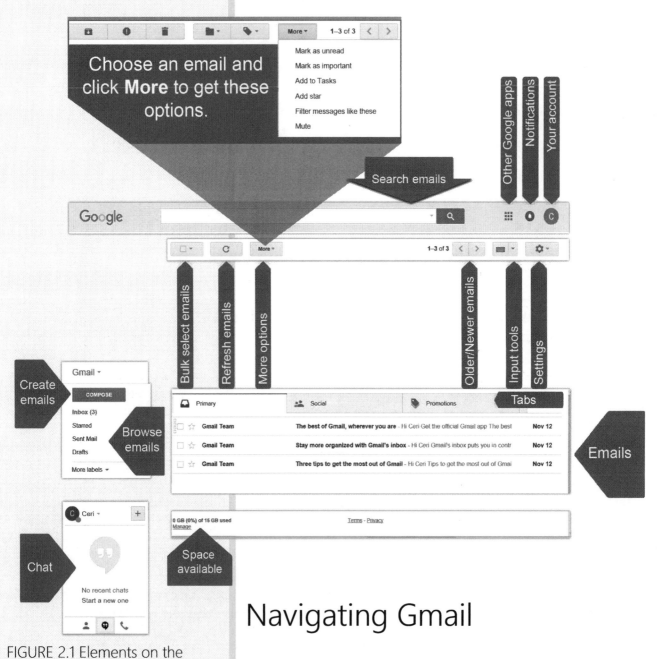

FIGURE 2.1 Elements on the page.

Navigating Gmail

Navigating Gmail can be done from three places, the top navigation section which includes the search bar, the Gmail specific functions directly underneath the navigation bar and the side navigation panel. Please see the following sections for more information.

The top navigation bars

There are two navigation bars on the top of the screen. I will call the first one, *Account navigation* and the second one the *Gmail-specific top navigation bar*. I have to apologise for the mouthful but it seems the most obvious way to differentiate between the two bars.

Account navigation

Search

Beside the Google logo, you will always see the search bar at the top in Gmail. You can search for your emails and it will even search through your attachments for you.

Sometimes you need some more control over searching your emails in Gmail. Google has given you more options

FIGURE 2.2 The search box.

but you have to look for it. Inside the search bar next to the magnifying glass there is a little arrow pointing down. Click on this to get more search options.

App launcher

When you press on the squares (on the top right of your screen), you will be given the option to go to other Google services like Docs, Slides, Drive and Maps etc. You can add more apps to the initial list and re-arrange them as you prefer them laid out. For example, you may use Gmail and Docs more than any other Google service. The icons can be moved around so they appear at the top.

FIGURE 2.3 The Apps button.

FIGURE 2.4 Notifications

FIGURE 2.5 Your Account.

FIGURE 2.6 Bulk select your emails.

Notifications

These are Google+ and photo notifications. You can safely ignore these if you have no intention of joining Google+ or using Google Photos.

Account

Here you can change your account options, find out about Google's privacy policy and update your Google settings. This is where you can add or change your profile picture and manage your security settings for Google.

Gmail-specific top navigation

Bulk select emails

You may want to select more than one email at a time. Possibly to move them to a folder/label, declare them as spam or just delete them. Gmail gives you several options to select a few emails all at the same time. At the time of writing these were, **all**, **none**, **read**, **unread**, **starred** and **unstarred**. If you search for a keyword then you can use these options for even more control. For example if you search for a company name, you can then click on unread to see all the emails you haven't had a chance to read yet.

Refresh emails

Click this button to see if you have any new emails. I do this a lot.

More options

At the top of the overview graphic at the beginning of this chapter you can see another set of options that do not appear unless you have clicked on an email.

When you click **More** you can mark all as read but if you

24

want the other options they will only appear when you check the box of one or more emails.

The new options are:

- archive
- report spam
- delete
- move to
- labels
- even more settings

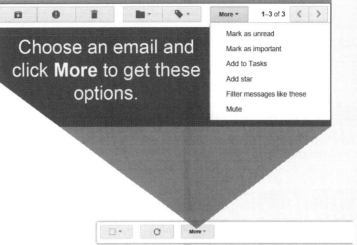

Choose an email and click **More** to get these options.

FIGURE 2.7 The more button.

The settings when you click on **More** include:

- Mark as unread
- Mark as important
- Add to Tasks
- Add Star
- Filter messages like these
- Mute

Older/newer arrows

Use these arrows to browse pages of your emails in the order that you receive them whether older or newer. You can set how many emails appear in each page in the settings.

Input tools

Google input tools are useful if you need to type in different languages or you need to have a custom dictionary. You may never need to use this option but if you have friends with unusual names like mine it is useful to add their names into your dictionary so Google knows it is a name you want to type and it is not just a typo.

FIGURE 2.8 Input tools.

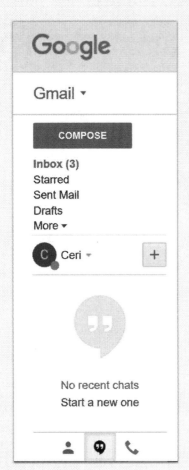

FIGURE 2.9 The side navigation bar.

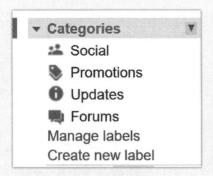

FIGURE 2.10 Click on categories to get to your Social, Promotions, Updates and Forums inboxes.

Settings

Please see *Chapter 11: Under the Hood - Gmail Settings* for more information on this.

Side navigation

The navigation bar on the left, as seen at the beginning of this chapter, holds the main means of finding your emails. If you have made any labels/folders, they will appear in here. If you cannot see them, click on **More** labels or use your mouse and click on the line directly below the labels you can see and drag it down to see more.

The Google Logo

Wherever you are on Gmail, if you click on the Google logo it will take you to the Gmail homepage.

Gmail (includes home button, Contacts and Tasks)

At the top of this section you will see Gmail (under the Google logo). Clicking on this will show you **Gmail**, **Contacts** and **Tasks**. Clicking on Gmail will take you back to the inbox (as will the Google logo), please see *Chapter 6 Your Contacts* for more information on managing you contacts and *Chapter 14 Tasks* for how you can use tasks.

Compose

Click on this button to start a new email. Please take a look at *Chapter 5 Sending and Receiving Emails* for more detail on this.

Browse your emails with Labels

The options that come 'out of the box' are **Inbox, Starred, Sent mail, Drafts** and **More** labels. When you click on

More, you will get the additional options of **Important, Chats, All Mail, Spam, Trash** and **Categories**. When you click on **Categories** you will be given **Social, Promotions, Updates** and **Forums**.

Below Categories are **Manage labels** and **Create new label.** For detailed information on how to use labels, please jump ahead to *Chapter 7 Email Organization with Labels.*

Tabs

Google has set up four tabs, which are really just labels but they control them. These are **Social, Promotions, Updates** and **Forums**. Google will try to categorise your emails for you if you choose to use these. You can turn these off if you want finer control but if you are starting out, it can be useful to separate your Facebook, Linkedin, Twitter or even Google+ notifications from your usual email. You can do this yourself by using filters. See *Chapter 8 Filters and Blocked Addresses* on how to do this.

Emails

Your emails will be in the second pane under Google's tabs. You can select an email by clicking anywhere on it or checking the box next to it. Beside this you will see who the email is from and then what the email is about. The final information you will see is the date you received the email.

Chat

Use this section to chat to your friends on Gmail. Sometimes it is quicker to get an answer when you send a chat message over an email message. This is a way of keeping a record of your chats in your email as your chats are searchable when you search in Gmail. You can turn this off in the settings.

Did you know...

You can save space in your Google account by saving your attachments to Drive in the Google formats. They ignore space taken up by files that are in the Google Sheets and Docs file types.

If you are saving your photos in Google Drive (remember space used there affects your Gmail account), you can choose to save your photos as high quality not original quality in photos.google.com/settings. There is free unlimited storage for your photos that are under 16 megapixels. If your photos are bigger than this Google will convert them so they are smaller. The same applies to videos which have less than a resolution of 1080p.

Space available

Google gives you 15 Gigabytes of space over your whole Google account. This is used up over all their services including Gmail, Drive, Docs, Sheets etc. If you are running out of space, it is a good idea to check your other Google apps such as Google Photos as well as attachments in your email account.

Chapter summary

If you are logged in to any Google service, the top-right of your browser window will show you which Google account you are logged in to, a menu to quickly navigate to other Google services, Google+/photo notifications and access to your overall account settings such as security and privacy options.

The Gmail specific options in the top navigation include archiving, reporting spam and moving your emails into different labels/folders.

Below the main navigation window on the left-hand side is the main navigation which contains your labels. These are like folders but you can have one email in several places without duplication. There is still only one email but you can see it from different places. Be careful if you delete an email, it will be deleted from everywhere!

If you would like to use the chat functionality of Gmail then that is located at the bottom left of the window.

All your emails will be listed in the main window beside the left navigation pane unless you have archived your email. For clarification, if you archive an email, all this does is remove the **inbox** label from an email. Unless you assign a label/folder to your email it will be in limbo but you can find it again by clicking on **All Mail**.

You can check how much space you have left in your Google account by looking at the bottom of the page.

Chapter 03

Getting Started

What to expect in this chapter:

- First steps in setting up your Google account

- Adding your profile picture

- Importing mail and contacts

- Logging in

- Adding Google and Gmail as your homepage

- Reading emails

- Gmail's category inboxes (tabs)

- Turning chat off

Now that you have your new Google account, you can set it up so that your profile is up-to-date (handy for when people who have you in their contacts can see who you are) and you can import your mail and contacts from other service providers.

Adding your profile picture

Gmail is only a part of the office applications suite that Google gives you for free. When you create a Google Profile it will be used across all Google services. This means that if you collaborate with someone in Google Docs or Sheets they can see a little picture of you next to changes you make or even when you are currently working on it. The information can also be used in Google+ but you can choose not to make you profile public if you so wish. Your picture can also end up on emails that you send to people who use Gmail and even on your friend's phones in your contact information (when they put your email address into the contact information).

Stop! Do you have Adobe Flash installed?

On some browsers you may need Adobe Flash to be installed to add your profile picture. Some of the elements won't appear on the page and the **Set as profile photo** button won't work without it either. Here is the briefest of guides for adding Adobe Flash to your computer.

1. Go to https://get.adobe.com/flashplayer/
2. Uncheck the optional offers (unless you really want them)
3. Click on Install now
4. Save the installer file on to your computer
5. Run the installer file on your computer (left click on the file and click OK)
6. Restart your browser

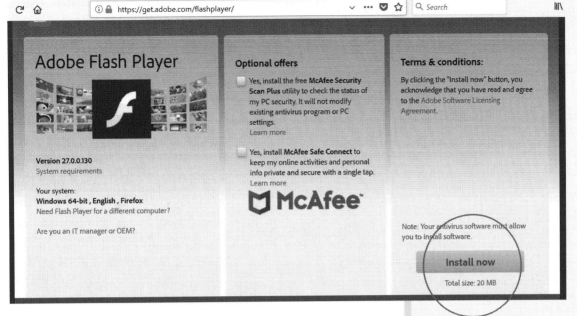

Adding your profile picture

To upload a profile picture on to Google, first click on the initial of your name at the top right of your browser. In the box that loads, click on **Change** inside the big circle with your initial in it.

There are four ways you can add your photo to your account. These are upload a photo, look through your photos held in your Google account, choose photos of yourself in your or others' Google accounts and you can take a photo using your web camera.

A quick note about your profile picture. What you choose to have as your photo is of course entirely up to you but if you are using your new email account for business then choosing a business appropriate photo might be the way to go. If you want to be more anonymous on the internet, a lovely picture of your pet, a photo of you in shadow or even an illustration could be more appropriate. Basically think about how you want the profile connected to this account to be viewed by the world.

Upload a photo from your computer.

1. Click on your initial on the top right of the screen
2. Click on **Change** (inside the circle)

FIGURE 3.1 Installing Adobe Flash.

FIGURE 3.2 Where to go to add your profile picture

31

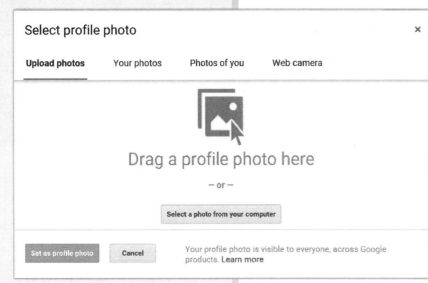

FIGURE 3.3 Ways to upload your profile picture.

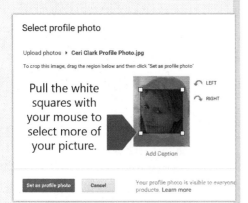

FIGURE 3.4 Edit your picture.

3. Click on **Select a photo from your computer**

4. Browse the files on your computer for a suitable picture or a flattering photo and select it. Click **Open** and the picture will start uploading. You will be given the option to edit your photo before it becomes live

5. Reposition and move the squares with your mouse until you have the picture how you want it. The left and right buttons to the right of your profile picture rotates it left or right

6. Click on **Set as profile photo**. Please note that if the '**Set as profile picture**' button doesn't work, you may need to install Adobe Flash and/or use another browser. Once the button is pressed your picture will replace your initial at the top right of your browser

Choose a photo from 'Your photos'

1. Click on your initial on the top right of the screen
2. Click on **Change** (inside the circle)
3. Click on **Your photos**
4. Choose from photos from your phone, Google+ or somewhere else on your Google account
5. Click on **Set as profile photo**. If this step does not work, try a different browser. Chrome or Firefox are recommended

Choose a photo from 'Photos of you'

1. Click on your initial on the top right of the screen
2. Click on **Change** inside the circle
3. Click on **Photos of you**
4. Choose from photos from your account or from other users of Google+. If you do decide to use any

of these pictures make sure you have the permission to have them as your Google Profile photo

5. Click on **Set as profile photo**. If this step does not work, try a different browser. Chrome or Firefox are recommended

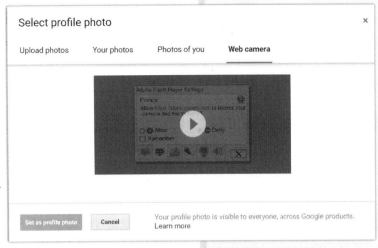

FIGURE 3.5 Click on the play button to allow Flash to work.

Choose a photo using your web camera

Last but not least you can use your web camera to create your profile photo.

1. Click on your initial on the top right of the screen

2. Click on **Change** (inside the circle)

3. Click on **Web camera**

4. Click on the play button in the middle of the screen

5. Allow it to access your camera and microphone. Without allowing this, you can't take a picture with your camera. I *never* choose **Remember** for this kind of thing as I want to know what is using my camera but then I can be known as slightly paranoid!

FIGURE 3.6 Allow Google to access your camera.

6. Click on the red button with the camera symbol and **Take a snapshot** written on it. You can do this as many times until you get the result you want. When you are ready. Google will keep the last four photos that you take and you can choose from them

7. When you have found the perfect picture, click on **Set as profile photo**. If you change your mind and want to finish it later, click on **Cancel**. You can add a profile picture at any time

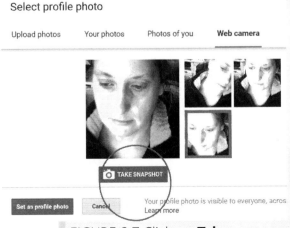

FIGURE 3.7 Click on **Take snapshot** when you are ready.

Importing mail and contacts

Did you know...

Other email providers may stop you from importing information as a security feature. Yahoo is one of these. If you want to import emails and contacts from Yahoo *and it is not working* then you will have to enable a feature to allow this to work. Here's how to do this:

- Login in to Yahoo mail

- Click on your name at the top right of the screen

- Click on **Account info**

- Click on **Account security**

- Enable **Allow apps that use less secure sign-in**

The steps listed should now work.

If you have another email account you may want to import all your previous email into your brand new Google account. Google can import all your old emails and any new ones that come into your old account. This comes in very handy if you have more than one email account but you want to check them from the one location. They can also import just your old emails, this would be useful if you just want to have Gmail going forward.

Importing you contacts from AOL, Hotmail, Yahoo! or any other webmail or POP3 accounts is simple with Gmail.

1. From your Gmail homepage, click on the gear wheel on the top right of your screen

2. In the drop-down menu, choose **Settings** which is near the bottom of the list. Please take a look at *figure 3.11* for a visual guide

3. Click on **Accounts and Import** (under **Settings**). This will take you to a page where you can change your password. The second option is **Import mail and contacts**

4. Click on **Import mail and contacts**

5. Type in your email address in the box that loads and click **Continue**

6. Enter your password for you other email address in the box and click on **Continue**

7. You will be asked to sign into your other email account to confirm it's actually you trying to import your email and not someone else. Click on **Continue**. You will be taken to your previous email such as Yahoo to sign in

8. Sign in and agree to the transfer of email and contacts (*see figure 3.16*). If you are still happy to do this, click on **Agree**

9. The next window to load will be a confirmation that your two accounts are connected. You will need to close the window to carry on

10. Back in Google, you will be asked what you want to import. There are three options and you can choose to check one or all the boxes. The importing of your

34

data is done by another party so you cannot have your email imported for more than 30 days, however you can have your mail brought into Google indefinitely through the settings which I will explain later. I would therefore not bother with the third option as you might get your emails duplicated

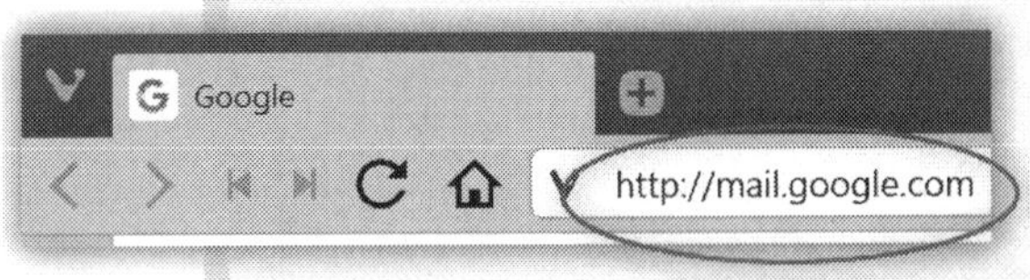

FIGURE 3.8 The URL (address) bar.

As the Yahoo account was new and created specifically for this book, my emails and contacts were imported within seconds. The time it takes to import your mail and contacts will vary depending on how many you have to transfer.

As you can see there are three emails even before you've told all your best mates about your new address and imported your old email. These hold links to customizing the look and feel, importing your contacts and old email from other email services and using your mobile phone to see your email.

Logging in

Say sometime has flown by and you haven't checked your email. You click open your browser, probably Internet Explorer, Chrome, Firefox or even Vivaldi. The horror, it's logged you out, how do I check it now?

FIGURE 3.9 Enter your email address or phone number.

Going directly there

Depending on if you bought this as a paperback or e-book, you could type in the following website address or highlight and copy it

https://mail.google.com

...and paste it into the address bar. Press **Enter** on your keyboard (otherwise known as Return) and you will be taken directly there.

Type in your email and click on **Next**. A new box will load inviting you to type in your password. As you type it will be hidden by dots in case there is anyone behind you, having a snoop.

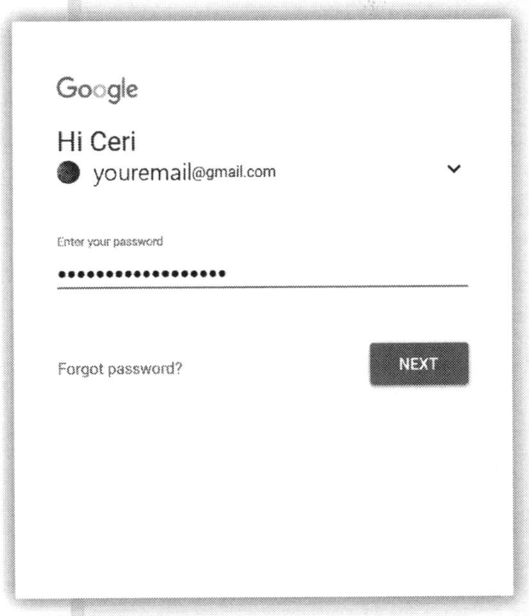

FIGURE 3.10 Enter your password and click *Next*.

Visual guide to importing mail and contacts

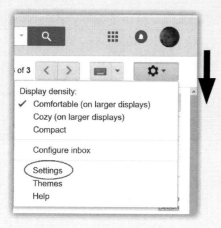

FIGURE 3.11 Where to find the settings.

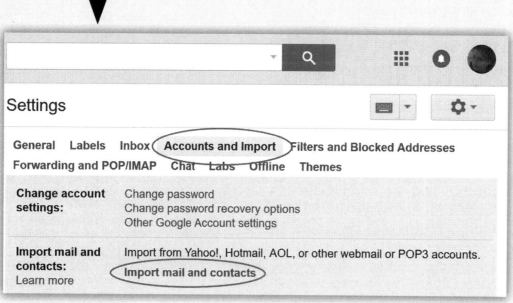

FIGURE 3.12 Where to find Accounts and Import and Import mail and contacts.

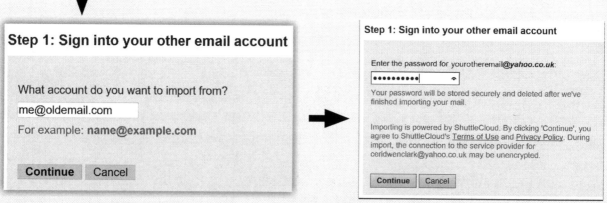

FIGURE 3.13 Type in your email address.

FIGURE 3.14 Enter your password.

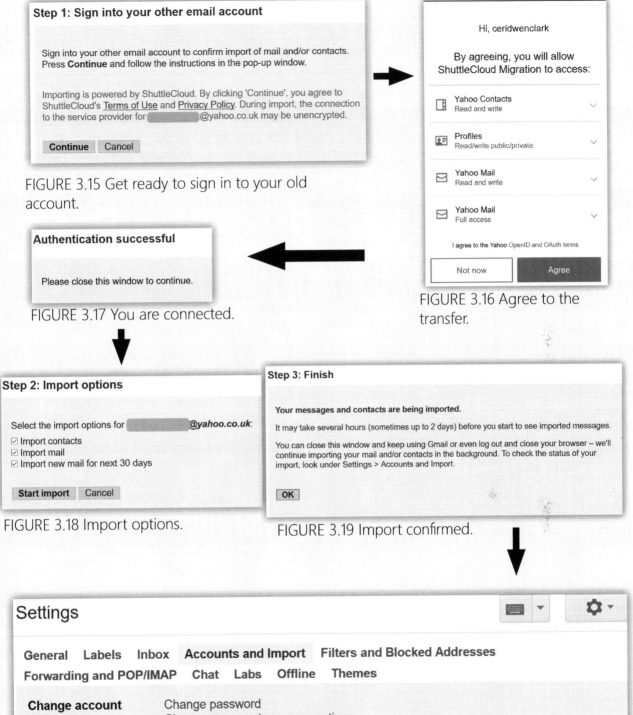

Step 1: Sign into your other email account

Sign into your other email account to confirm import of mail and/or contacts. Press **Continue** and follow the instructions in the pop-up window.

Importing is powered by ShuttleCloud. By clicking 'Continue', you agree to ShuttleCloud's Terms of Use and Privacy Policy. During import, the connection to the service provider for ⬚⬚⬚⬚@yahoo.co.uk may be unencrypted.

Continue Cancel

FIGURE 3.15 Get ready to sign in to your old account.

Hi, ceridwenclark

By agreeing, you will allow ShuttleCloud Migration to access:

Yahoo Contacts
Read and write

Profiles
Read/write public/private

Yahoo Mail
Read and write

Yahoo Mail
Full access

I agree to the Yahoo OpenID and OAuth terms

Not now   Agree

FIGURE 3.16 Agree to the transfer.

Authentication successful

Please close this window to continue.

FIGURE 3.17 You are connected.

Step 2: Import options

Select the import options for ⬚⬚⬚⬚ *@yahoo.co.uk*:
☑ Import contacts
☑ Import mail
☑ Import new mail for next 30 days

Start import Cancel

FIGURE 3.18 Import options.

Step 3: Finish

Your messages and contacts are being imported.

It may take several hours (sometimes up to 2 days) before you start to see imported messages.

You can close this window and keep using Gmail or even log out and close your browser – we'll continue importing your mail and/or contacts in the background. To check the status of your import, look under Settings > Accounts and Import.

OK

FIGURE 3.19 Import confirmed.

Settings

General   Labels   Inbox   Accounts and Import   Filters and Blocked Addresses
Forwarding and POP/IMAP   Chat   Labs   Offline   Themes

Change account settings:	Change password Change password recovery options Other Google Account settings	
Import mail and contacts: Learn more	⬚⬚⬚⬚ **@yahoo.co.uk** Importing – It may take several hours (sometimes up to 2 days) before you start to see imported messages. You can leave this page and the import will continue. **Import from another address**	stop

FIGURE 3.20 The import progress can be seen in **Accounts and Import.**

FIGURE 3.21 The Menu button in Chrome.

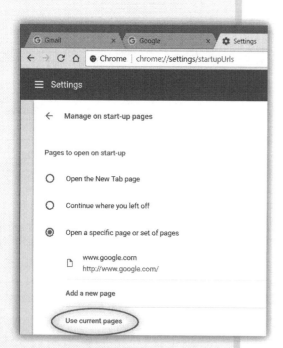

FIGURE 3.22 Use current pages.

Adding Google and Gmail as your homepage

If the first thing you do each day is check your Gmail account and maybe do a search in Google, I recommend setting Gmail and Google as two separate tabs as your home pages. This way when you first open your browser these pages will load automatically.

On Microsoft internet Explorer

If you are using Internet Explorer, these are the steps to follow:

1. Open two tabs, one showing Gmail and the other Google search, (this will of course work for any website that you want to open each time you open your browser)
2. Click on the little gear wheel on the top right of your browser window
3. Choose **Internet Options**
4. Choose **Use current** in the Home page section
5. Once you have done this click on **Apply** then **OK**

These two pages will be the first pages you see when you load your browser. Selecting the little house icon on the top right of your browser will also bring up these pages from now on.

On Google's Chrome

1. Open two tabs, one showing Gmail and the other Google search, (this will of course work for any website that you want to open each time you open your browser)
2. Click on the menu button on the top right of your window (three vertical dots)

3. Choose **Settings**
4. Scroll down to the **On start-up** section and click on **Restore tabs or open specific pages**
5. Click on **Use current pages**

The pages will now be set. You can check it by closing and reopening the browser. Every time you open your browser, these two tabs will load, saving you time.

On Firefox

1. Open two tabs, one showing Gmail and the other Google search, (this will of course work for any website that you want to open each time you open your browser)
2. Click on the menu button on the top right of your window. This looks like three horizontal lines (*see figure 3.23*)
3. Choose **Options** and then
4. Choose **Current Pages** in the **Home Page** section

The pages will now be set. You can check it by closing and reopening the browser. Every time you open your browser, these two tabs will load, saving you time.

FIGURE 3.23 The Menu button in Firefox.

Reading emails

This is the reason you created the account, right? Well this couldn't be simpler. As with every other email service out there, you just click anywhere on the email. The emails are displayed with who sent it first, the subject (what the

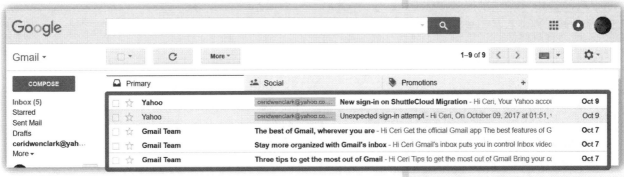

FIGURE 3.24 Click on any row in the box to read that email.

FIGURE 3.25 Trash/bin symbol for deleting emails.

email is about) and then the date it arrived. I'm interested in looking at my emails on my mobile so I click on the **The best of Gmail, wherever you are** email.

Images are sometimes blocked by Google. This is done to protect your computer but you can change this by changing the settings. If you would like to always see the images in your emails, got to the **gear wheel** (top right of your screen), **Settings**, then in the **General** tab scroll down to **Images** and choose **Always display external images**.

If you are happier to choose which images you want Google to display then go to the same place as above (**Gear wheel** > **Settings** > **Images**) and choose **Ask before displaying external images**. Whenever Google stops you seeing an image you will get a message underneath the sender's email address that the images have been hidden. Click on **Display images below** to see the email as it was meant to be viewed.

Once you have read the email, you can click on Inbox, the Gmail logo, archive or delete to send you right back to the home screen.

Notice that once you have read an email, (*see figure 3.24*) it is no longer bold.

To delete the email, click on the small box to the left of the email and then click on the picture of a bin/trash can above it. If you hover your mouse over the pictures, a little message pops up telling you what the picture means. I will go into more detail in the next chapter.

Viewing attachments

With Gmail you can look at attachments from right inside your browser. This means that if you don't have the software on your computer then you can still see most documents. You can view these documents as long

FIGURE 3.26 Download, edit or save emailed documents.

as you have a) access to the internet and b) access to a browser.

Figure 3.26 shows how Google displays what documents are attached to the email. To view the options available, you will need to hover your mouse over the pictures. As you can see, you can download and save them individually or all of the attachments at the same time. If the document is compatible with Google Docs like Microsoft Word then you will also be given the option to edit the file within Google Docs. This means that you can look at and edit Microsoft Word documents without having Microsoft Word on your computer.

You can also get a preview of images by clicking on the images and they will load in your browser. If Google does not support the attachment file type, for example, a Mobi file, you can download the file on to your computer and use software from there. In this case Kindle for PC or Calibre.

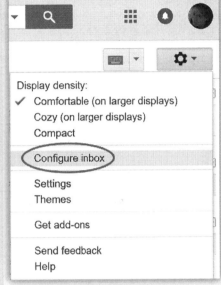

FIGURE 3.27 You can get to Gmail category inbox settings from the Gear Wheel menu.

Gmail's category inboxes (tabs)

Google has a set of category inboxes which can be used to automatically categorise your emails as they come in. They will appear above your message list on the homepage and all you need to do is click on the tab to see the emails.

You can activate or remove Gmail category inboxes (which appear as tabs above your message list) from two places:

> Location 1. Gear Wheel > **Configure inbox**
>
> Location 2. Gear Wheel > **Settings > Inbox (as long as Default is selected in the first option)**

In location 2, you can only add or remove inboxes from

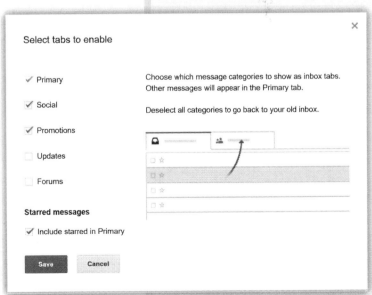

FIGURE 3.28 You can add or remove inboxes/tabs from the Gear Wheel menu.

Did you know

Sometimes emails are put into the wrong category. You can easily tell Google where the correct place to put these emails by the following two methods:

1. Drag the email from its current location and 'dump' it in the tab (located above the messages list) that you want.

2. a) right-click on the offending email

b) then, click on **Move to tab** and choose the correct category. *See figure 3.29.*

In either method, Gmail will confirm that the move has taken place at the top of the web page. Gmail will also ask if you want this to happen to future messages as well. Click **Yes** if you do, **ignore** it if you don't.

the first location. If you want to configure them, you will need to go to the Inbox settings as explained in *Chapter 11 Under the hood - Gmail Settings* in the **Inbox** section.

The primary tab

Your primary tab is the first tab you will see when you open your inbox. It should have all the emails that you or Google thinks are important to you. If Google cannot classify emails, then they will go into here.

The social tab

Google will put any emails from social networks in this tab to stop them cluttering up your primary inbox. These can be from Facebook and Twitter to Goodreads.

The promotions tab

The promotions tab is for all those emails offering you deals on your favorite stores that you signed up for in the past. If you don't want these but you remember signing up in the first place then you can usually unsubscribe by going to the bottom of the open email and locating and clicking on the word **unsubscribe**. If you didn't sign up for the emails then feel free to mark them as spam. There are instructions for how to do this in the next chapter (*Chapter 4 Security*).

The updates and forums tabs

The emails categorized as updates are usually confirmations, receipts, bills, and statements and emails put into the forums category are usually from mailing lists or forums.

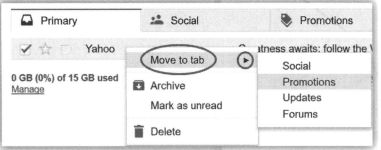

FIGURE 3.29 Move emails to a different tab.

Turn off Chat

If you are new to Google then there is plenty of time to find out more but to reduce the risk of information overload I recommend you turn off **Chat**.

You can always reactivate it later, but for now there's so much to concentrate on.

First, go to the gear wheel at the top right of the screen, this is the main settings button, and then click on **Settings**.

A dropdown menu will appear when it is clicked on allowing you to choose tabs which run along the top of the screen. Please take a look at *figure 3.28* for where these tabs are and where **Chat** is within these settings. Please be aware that if you make your browser window smaller then Chat may end up appearing on a second line but it is fourth from the end.

Go to the circled location labelled **Chat** (as seen in *figure 3.30*) to get all the settings relevant to Chat. Turn chat off by choosing **Chat off** and then clicking **Save Changes** at the bottom of the screen.

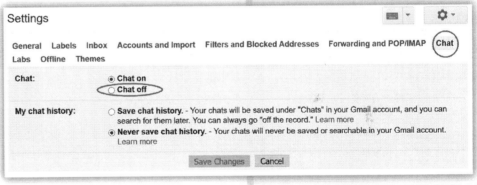

FIGURE 3.30 Where to find Chat in the settings & where to turn it off.

Reactivating Chat

If you would like to do this later, follow the steps in turning it off but choose **Chat on**.

Chapter summary

This chapter was all about giving you a head start on the basics. How to add your profile picture, importing your mail and contacts from your other email addresses, how to get to Gmail, reading your emails and turning off chat.

There is also a section on using Gmail's category inboxes which appear as tabs above your message lists. This section covered what they are and how to turn them on and off. A tip in the side bar explains how to quickly move an email which has gone into the wrong tab.

While some of these may not be essential, they will make your experience more enjoyable while you learn how to get the most out of what Gmail has to offer.

Chapter 04

Security

What to expect in this chapter:

- Passwords

- How to set up 2-step verification

- Spam and phishing

Securing your Google account is very important. The sum of all your emails, posts, contacts and other data can help someone to take advantage of you (and even your friends) or use your details for their own use. Identity theft is a growing problem on the internet and you need to protect yourself as much as possible.

Passwords

I go into detail about this in *Chapter 1* in the section called *Choosing your password*. Please read this for ways of choosing your password.

Changing your password

To change your password at any time, go to the settings page (the gear icon on the top right of the screen), then **Accounts and Import**. The Change Password link is the first item in the page as seen below.

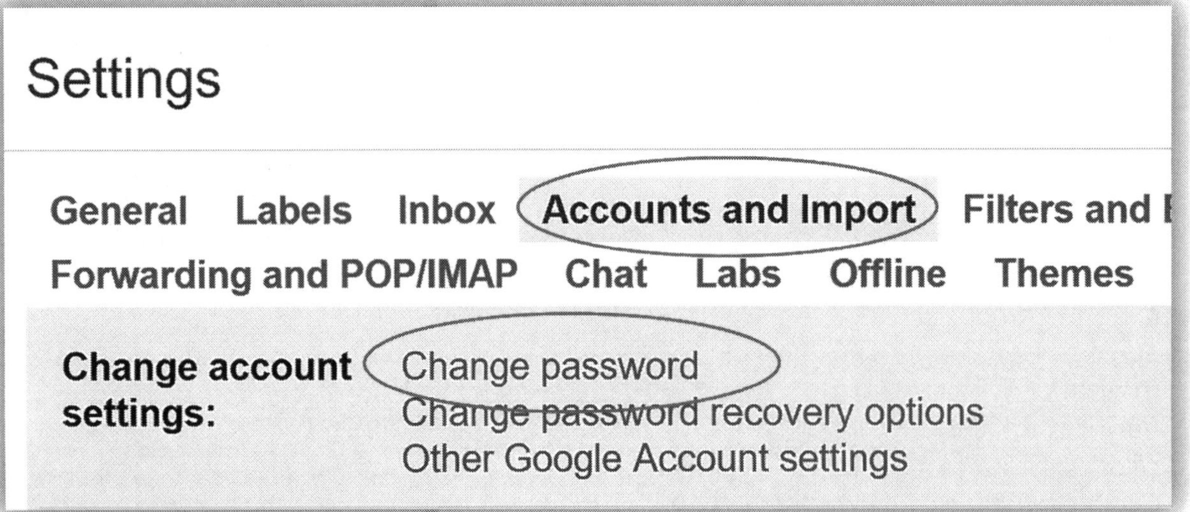

Did you know...

You can also change your Google/Gmail Account password by going to:

1. **Profile picture**
2. **My Account**
3. **Sign-in and security**
4. **Password**

Settings

General	Labels	Inbox	**Accounts and Import**	Filters and I

Forwarding and POP/IMAP   Chat   Labs   Offline   Themes

Change account settings: Change password
Change password recovery options
Other Google Account settings

FIGURE 4.1 Where to go to change your password.

Two-factor authentication

Changing your password regularly is a good way of securing access to your account, but remembering hundreds of passwords, constantly changing, can be impossible. Google's two-step verification (also known as two-factor authentication) can be an elegant solution to this for access to their website and services.

2-step verification/authentication is an extra step to make sure that access to your information, files and folders is restricted to you. Instead of relying just on a password (which can be discovered by nefarious means by hackers), a second device is used which you always have on you such as a phone or tablet computer. Any would-be infiltrator, bent on your destruction would need to have your password AND your phone to gain access to your account.

When you setup 2-factor authentication, you can set a computer to be trusted while logging in. This can save you a lot of time but if for any reason you want to reset your access on all your devices, you can go to your 2-step verification page and click on **REVOKE ALL** under **Devices you trust** (at the bottom of the page) for peace of mind.

How to setup 2-step verification on Google

1. Go to your profile picture and click on it followed by **My Account**

2. Click on **Sign-in & securi-ty** (the first box)

3. In the section labelled **Signing into Google**, look for the box head-ed **Password & sign-in method**. Click on **2-Step Verification**. Once you click on **GET STARTED**, Google will go through the following steps with you

4. First verify it is you by typing in your password and then click **NEXT**

5. Type in your mobile phone number. You can choose to get this by text message or phone call. Click on **NEXT**

6. Type in the code that Google sends you. If you didn't receive it you can ask for it to be sent again.

Did you know...

To get to your 2-step verification page go to:

1. **Profile picture**
2. **My Account**
3. **Sign-in and se-curity**
4. **2-step verifica-tion**

Ceri Clark
cericlark2018@gmail.com
Privacy

Change

My Account

Add account   Sign out

CLICK HERE

THEN HERE

FIGURE 4.2 Your security options are located under **My Account**.

Click **NEXT**

7. If you are happy with turning this feature on, then click on **TURN ON**

Backup options

Life happens and there may be a time you can't get into your account. You may lose your phone or it might be stolen. You might even forget your password. If you don't choose one of Google's backup or alternative second step options you could lose access to your Google account. This wouldn't be just your email but all your documents, spreadsheets, photos. It could be disastrous. Luckily there is a way to solve this but only if you activate the backup options in advance before something goes wrong. You should use at least one of these options. You cannot use Google Prompt *and* the security key so if you want to use the security key bear that in mind.

Backup codes

The most important of these methods is the backup codes. These are one-time codes that you can use to get into your account. Print them out and put them somewhere safe. You may never need them but it's almost guaranteed that if you don't have them you will need them at some point.

Go to the 2-step verification section of Google and choose **SET UP**. If you are not sure how to get there:

1. In any Google Service, click on your account picture on the top right of the screen
2. Click on **My Account**
3. Click on **Sign-in and security**
4. In the section labelled **Signing into Google**, look for the box headed **Password & sign-in method**. Click on **2-Step Verification**
5. Prove who you are by tapping in your password
6. Type in the code that Google sends you
7. In the **Set up alternative second step** section look for **Backup codes** and click on **SET UP**

48

8. Download the codes and save them to your computer or print them out to store or carry with you

When Google asks for a code you can use any of these that you generated once. Cross them out once you've used them so you know they are inactive. You can get new codes by clicking on **GET NEW CODES** at the bottom of the screen above **CLOSE**, **DOWNLOAD** and **PRINT**.

If you lose your backup codes...

If you lose your backup codes you will have to stop them working and get new ones.

1. In any Google Service, click on your account picture on the top right of the screen
2. Click on **My Account**
3. Click on **Sign-in and security**
4. In the section labelled **Signing into Google**, look for the box headed **Password & sign-in method**. Click on **2-Step Verification**
5. Prove who you are by tapping in your password
6. Type in the code that Google sends you
7. In the **Your second step** section look for Backup codes and click on **SHOW CODES**
8. Click on **GET NEW CODES** at the bottom of the screen above **CLOSE**, **DOWNLOAD** and **PRINT**

By getting new codes, the old codes will stop working automatically. They become useless.

Google Prompt

Every time you login to Google from an unknown computer or after a period of time, you will be asked for a verification code that Google will send to your mobile phone. This can be very time-consuming and sometimes, if I'm honest, a little annoying. Google has taken this on board and offered the phone prompt option. Before you do this, make sure you have a screen lock on your mobile phone or anyone will be able to just tap the prompt when

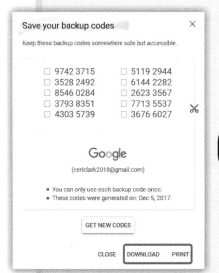

Save your backup codes ✕

Keep these backup codes somewhere safe but accessible.

☐ 9742 3715   ☐ 5119 2944
☐ 3528 2492   ☐ 6144 2282
☐ 8546 0284   ☐ 2623 3567
☐ 3793 8351   ☐ 7713 5537
☐ 4303 5739   ☐ 3676 6027

Google

{cericlark2018@gmail.com}

▪ You can only use each backup code once.
▪ These codes were generated on: Dec 5, 2017.

GET NEW CODES

CLOSE   DOWNLOAD   PRINT

FIGURE 4.3 Download or print your backup codes.

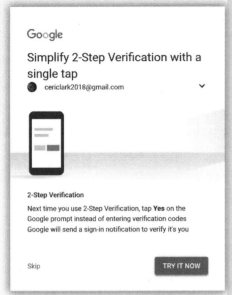

FIGURE 4.4 If you have your Google account on your phone (and it is connected to the internet), Google will automatically find it.

FIGURE 4.5 Let Google know it is you by clicking on **YES**.

you are not looking.

1. In any Google Service, click on your account picture on the top right of the screen
2. Click on **My Account**
3. Click on **Sign-in and security**
4. In the section labelled **Signing into Google**, look for the box headed **Password & sign-in method**. Click on **2-Step Verification**
5. Prove who you are by tapping in your password
6. Type in the code that Google sends you
7. In the **Set up alternative second step** section look for **Google Prompt** and click on **ADD PHONE**
8. Click on **GET STARTED**

You can do this with an Android phone or an iPhone. The next step is to add your phone. First, choose the type of phone you have. This, at the time of writing, works on Google's Android mobile phones and Apple's iPhone (5S or later). If you don't already have your Google account on your Android phone or the Google app on your iPhone, you will have to set these up before you start. If you have already added your account to your mobile phone, skip the next steps and go straight to Step 9 (after the instructions for adding Google accounts to your phone).

Adding your Google account to Android

a. Open the **Settings** section on your mobile phone
b. Press on **Accounts**
c. **Add Account**
d. Choose **Google** and sign in to your Google account

Adding your Google account to your iPhone

a. Visit the App Store
b. Find and install the Google app
c. Open the app and sign in to your Google account

Once your Google account is accessible on your phone, Google should be able to find it. Follow the instructions above to **GET STARTED** and then,

9. Click on **TRY IT NOW**

10. Click on **YES**

11. Click on **TURN IT ON**

Sign-in to Google with phone prompts with an older account

If you have been using Gmail for a while like me, then you might want to switch to phone prompts instead of typing in a code every now and again. It is so much quicker.

1. Go to your profile picture and click on it followed by **My Account**

2. Click on **Sign-in & security** (the first box)

3. In the box headed **Password & sign-in method**, click on **2-Step Verification**

4. Type in your password and click on **Next**

5. Click on **TRY IT NOW**

6. You will be prompted to click **yes** on your device. Don't worry if it suggests a device you don't usually use every day. When I trialled it for this book, it suggested my old tablet but the message appeared on my phone

7. You will be asked if you want to use Google Prompt for your device from now on. Click **TURN IT ON**

If you want to turn off phone prompts at any time, you can do this in **My Account** > **Sign-in & security** > **2-Step Verification**.

FIGURE 4.6 The final step to turn Google Prompt on is to click the blue button that says **TURN IT ON**.

The Authenticator App

The Authenticator app is an application that sits on your phone and works even if your phone is offline. It generates a one-time 6 digit code that will 'unlock' your account. You need to be quick though as these codes only last 60 seconds before they expire (text codes usually last for 5 minutes). It is essentially the same as if you had the code sent by text message. An alternative authenticator app is called Authy and this can be used for other sites as well. I will try to keep this book to within the Google ecosystem as much as I can

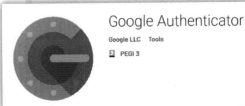

FIGURE 4.7 The Authenticator logo.

and although I personally use an app called Authy, these instructions are for Google Authenticator.

1. In any Google Service, click on your account picture on the top right of the screen
2. Click on **My Account**
3. Click on **Sign-in and security**
4. In the section labelled **Signing into Google**, look for the box headed **Password & sign-in method**. Click on **2-Step Verification**
5. Prove who you are by tapping in your password
6. In the **Set up alternative second step** section look for **Authenticator App** and click on **SET UP**
7. Let Google know whether you are using an Android device or an iPhone
8. Get the Authenticator App from the Play Store for Android or the App Store for Apple. Look for the logo at the beginning of this section
9. In the App select **Set up account**
10. Choose **Scan a barcode**
11. Hold your phone camera up to the screen until you see the QR code (grey square) on your phone
12. Click **next**
13. Type into the website the code that appears on your phone
14. Click on **VERIFY**
15. Click **DONE**

When you want to login to Google, open your app on the phone and type in the code when Google asks for one. While this is great for offline use, the Google Prompt option is faster and easier. You could consider this method as a secure backup of the backup.

Backup Phone

This option allows you have codes sent to a different phone. If you use someone else's phone make sure that you can trust them and you are happy for them to get into your Google account anytime they wish.

Should I use Google Prompt or Google Auth?

Please also note that this option disappears after setting up the first few 2-step verification options. This could be because the others are considered more secure. However, it can be an option if you would like to give your partner access to your account in the event something unfortunate happens. You can delegate access to your Gmail account so delegation may be a more suitable choice if you just want to give them access to see and answer emails. If it doesn't disappear and you want to use it, just reset 2-factor verification and turn the 2-factor authentication off and on.

Under **Backup phone**, click on **Add phone**, enter the phone number you want codes to go to and click **DONE**.

If you ever get locked out of your account, codes can now be sent to the alternative phone number.

Security Key

Security keys can be the most secure but be the least convenient. If you decide to use a security key, you will have to buy one that works with FIDO Universal 2nd Factor (U2F). You will always need to carry this key with you and you will have to use Google's Chrome browser for it to work. It won't work on some other browsers and if you use mail applications other than Gmail itself (or the Gmail website), it might not work either. The trade off is that it can provide better scam protection as they are encrypted and they won't work on bogus websites. Security keys work similarly to Google Authenticator in that they produce a random code that works to give you access to your Google Account but instead of in your mobile phone, it is a separate device.

If you decide that the better scam protection outweighs the disadvantages then please find the steps below to using one. Please also note, you can only use the Security key with the Chrome Browser, so you need to be using Chrome when setting it up as well as using it.

1. Search for *"FIDO U2F Security Key"* or *"Web authentication dongle"* in your favorite online store to buy one

Did you know...

FIDO is now also known as *web authentication*.

The Opera browser now supports the FIDO security key and from May 2018 Firefox will also support it.

2. In any Google Service, click on your account picture on the top right of the screen

3. Click on **My Account**

4. Click on **Sign-in and security**

5. In the section labelled **Signing into Google**, look for the box headed **Password & sign-in method**. Click on **2-Step Verification**

6. Prove who you are by tapping in your password

7. In the **Set up alternative second step** section look for **Security Key** and click on **ADD SECURITY KEY**

8. Follow the on-screen instructions

If your key does not have a button on it, then you will need to take the Key out of your USB port and back in again every time you use it.

Turning 2-Step Verification off

Google's 2-step verification is an important step in protecting your account but you may for some reason need to turn it off temporarily. If you feel you want to do this, here are the steps to achieve this.

1. In any Google Service, click on your account picture on the top right of the screen

2. Click on **My Account**

3. Click on **Sign-in and security**

4. In the section labelled **Signing into Google**, look for the box headed **Password & sign-in method**. Click on **2-Step Verification**

5. Prove who you are by tapping in your password

6. Type in the code that Google sends you

7. At the top of the page, click on the button that says, **TURN IT OFF**

Spam, Scams and Phishing

Spam, scams and phishing emails can be a security risk. They change all the time as the spammers/phishers get more sophisticated as time goes on but there are some things that make these messages stand out. This section includes just some of the things you can look out for and how to deal with them in Gmail

Recognizing spam, scams and phishing emails

Recognizing the type of emails that are spam, and/or contain scams and phishing attacks is the first step to dealing with them. Here are the top ways to recognize them.

It's too good to be true

If you receive an email from a Nigerian prince/princess letting you know that they are in trouble but they will give you several million but only if you give them your bank details - this can be a good indication.

Another famous email scam is a foreign lottery/ competition letting you know that you have won millions! This would be great, but if you have never bought a ticket, how likely is this actually to be true?

There are variations on these themes but they usually involve offering a large amount of money in unlikely circumstances.

Your friend is on vacation and asks you for money

This is a scam where your friend's email account has been hacked and an email then sent to you stating that s/he is in trouble on vacation and could you send them a couple of thousand to help him/her out? If you get any emails like this, check that they have actually gone on holiday first!

If you get any of these emails, tell your friend that his/ her account might have been hacked. The hacker may have deleted all sent emails so it may not be obvious to them that there was a problem. They will need to change their password straight away and maybe enable 2-step verification on their account.

A stranger sob story

A stranger is dying/ill/in trouble. Please send money quickly. I would ignore these emails. How did they even get your address? The sender is probably just sending these emails to random addresses to see if they can get anyone to reply.

An email sent to you by yourself

In the past I have sent emails to myself to remind me to do things. If there is one person I trust it is me! If I am very distracted it is not beyond the bounds of possibility that I could click on one of these emails by mistake. There is a scam where people have faked the email address so it looks like you have sent an email to yourself. Think before clicking on any links!

Bad grammar and spelling

A tell-tale sign of a malicious email is bad grammar and poor spelling. If you get an email with these features, handle with care.

Bank emails

Your bank will never ask you for personal information by email. They will also never give you a link to click on to log in. If you receive emails that ask for this, use a direct link you already have or your bank's mobile app. The web addresses are usually on letters and statements from your bank.

Some of these emails will say your account has been hacked, some money has gone missing or something along these lines. They will encourage you to click on a link in their email which will take you to a special website which will look like your bank's website but will be owned by the scammers. These emails are known as phishing emails. They will ask you to put in your username and password which they will then record. You will be redirected to your actual bank and you will probably not know what has happened until your real bank contacts you by phone or letter.

The way to avoid this is to never click on any link in an email that appears to be from your bank, but to go and have a look at your bank's website (or app) directly.

Reporting spam

Spam is the bane of all email users everywhere. Unwanted emails about medical aids, Nigerian princes needing help to take money from you or fake bank emails bring misery to billions. Spam is unsolicited bulk email, it may or may not be malicious. It can just be annoying. A form of spam is Malspam where you are sent a link to malware in your email. Once clicked the link will download malware on to your computer. This can result in your computer being taken over by the spammer. They can then ransom your computer (ask you for money to give you back control of your computer), or turn your computer into a 'bot' where they can send emails or even mine cryptocurrency in the background and make money from your computer while slowing it down. Fortunately Google h as one of the best spam filters on the web.

To find emails which may have been erroneously labelled spam, click on **Spam** on the left of the screen in the navigation bar. Re-label any emails you want to keep using the instructions in *Chapter 7 Email Organization with Labels.*

FIGURE 4.8 Report spam to Google by clicking on this button.

One of the reasons that Google is so good with spam is that there is a community effort to reduce it.

To mark an email as spam, click on the exclamation mark in the octagon symbol (as seen in *figure 4.8*).

It is always above your emails so you can let Google know the current email you are reading is spam.

Report phishing

There is another type of email which is sent with the sole

intent to cause either harm or take money from you. If you receive an email which you think is trying to trick you to going to a fake bank website that has 'slipped through the net', click on **Report phishing** in the menu that appears when you click on the arrow at the top right of each opened email (*figure 4.9* shows the location).

The unsubscribe link

Most of the time you will receive emails that you have signed up for in the past. You may not want them anymore but they are not spam as you originally asked for them. To stop receiving these, click on the **unsubscribe link** which is usually at the bottom of emails that have them.

Occasionally you will receive offers, promotions and other emails that you don't remember signing up for. If this happens to you, don't use the unsubscribe link. This is because these are spam messages used to try and get your details. Sometimes it is just to see if your email address is genuine. A good give-away for this is if your name is in the CC of the email (for example John Smith) but you can also see John A Smith, John B Smith, Jonnie smith etc. in there. They are trying every combination they can think of to get a hit. Other times it is to get other information such as a username or password. If you have different passwords for every website this is not a problem but a lot of people keep the same password for a lot of sites. Once they get hold of that password, they have access to those websites which could be banks or stores.

Chapter summary

It is important to look after your Google account which includes Gmail. Changing your password and enabling 2-step verification are important steps to protecting your account. There are a few options for 2-step verification from the convenient Google Prompt to the super secure Security Key (as long as you don't lose it!).

Recognising some of the most prevalent scams can also help secure not only your Google account but also any other website you visit online. When you register on

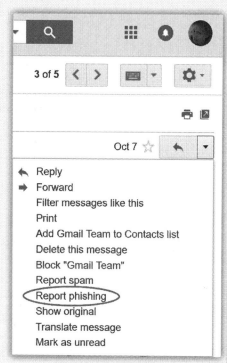

FIGURE 4.9 Report your email as a phishing attack from the email.

websites, emails acknowledging your registration and even password resets all go to your Gmail account. If an unauthorized person gets into your account, they can see what you signed up to and can reset passwords which could allow them to buy things using credit cards stored on retailer sites. Keeping them out with a good strong password, 2-step verification and avoiding scams can stop this happening.

04

Chapter 05

Sending and Receiving Emails

What to expect in this chapter:

- What are discussion threads

- How to reply and forward an email

- Composing and formatting emails

- Spell checking

- Deleting emails

Emails are dealt with a little differently in Gmail compared to some other email services. As long as the subject is the same, everything in one conversation is held in one place. No more searching through your Sent folder to find what you said! This section talks about how to send email but also how the discussion threads work.

Discussions

Discussion threads are conversations. Please see *figure 5.1* below for an example. If I have sent the email from this Gmail account then it will appear as '**me**'. Once read, it will go gray as illustrated below.

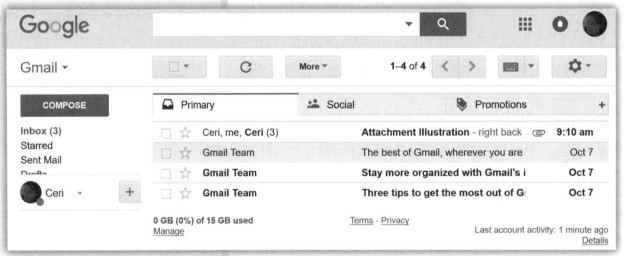

FIGURE 5.1 Example of a discussion thread.

Notice next to Ceri, the number lets me know how many emails are in the discussion. If anyone sends me an email later, it will revert to white (until I click on it) and the three will become a four. Next to the subject Google has also put some of the first line of the email visible, so I can decide if I want to read it or not.

The date will show you the date (or time if it was sent 'today') that an email was sent to you. If you respond to an email, then the date doesn't change but when you get a reply back it will do.

Click anywhere on the row and it will take you to the conversation.

Once you click on an email the thread will look like *figure 5.2*.

If you are not sure which email is the latest, look at the date at the top right of each email, which also tells you how long ago the email was sent. In this discussion thread example the first one arrived on October 18 and the next one was sent at 9:21 AM (0 minutes ago).

If you want to see more of the thread in one long message rather than clicking on each message, you can click on the three horizontal dots under the message you are viewing. You can see its location in *figure 5.2*. This has limited usage as the person who sent you the latest message may have deleted the thread in the email before they sent it to you. Don't rely on this as a complete record of your conversation. Your recipient is able to delete parts of the thread before they email it to you but they cannot delete emails in your email account. So if you are looking for something then it is best to search through your actual email rather than rely on a possibly trimmed discussion thread.

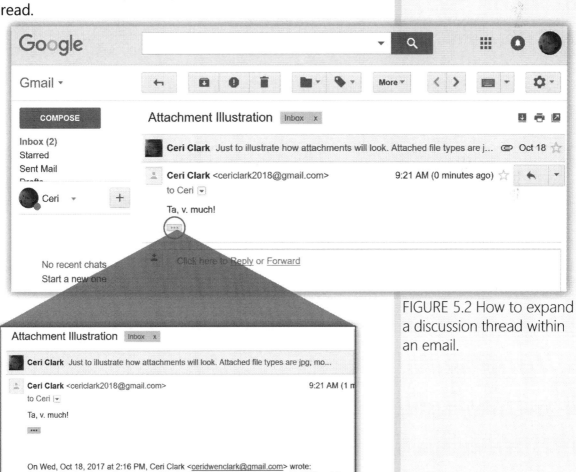

FIGURE 5.2 How to expand a discussion thread within an email.

Replying and forwarding an email

FIGURE 5.3 **Email options from Reply button.**

Replying to an email is as simple as clicking on Reply! Google has made this extra-easy by giving us two places to use this. At the top of the email on the right hand corner there is a grey box with an arrow in it as seen in *figure 5.3*. Clicking on this will bring up a dropdown list. The top option will be **Reply** and of course, there is always the Reply at the foot of each email beside **Forward**.

The reply box is illustrated in *figure 5.4*. Type in the white spaces and then click **Send**. Your email will automatically get saved by Google. If the internet cuts out or you forget to complete it, you will be able to find it again in **Drafts**, at the left of the screen.

The three dots at the bottom of the white box are previous emails. If you send an email without clicking on the three dots, the old conversation will still be sent to the email recipient. The only time it won't be included is if you click on the three dots and delete the conversations that appear. Remember that the other person will still have access to the actual emails you sent earlier. The only reason to send it is to make life easier for the person who will be reading your email. They can click on the three dots and quickly glance down to reacquaint themselves of the conversation without having to click in and out of older messages.

The box where you reply looks very simple but it is deceptive and once you delve into the buttons, there are a lot of options.

When you reply to an email the convention is to write your message above the email you are replying to. This means that your correspondent does not have to go looking for your answer. If you are replying to a friend then this does not matter as they will love you enough to go looking for your reply, but if you are using your email for business you do not want to annoy your customers/contacts before they have even read your message.

FIGURE 5.4 **The Reply box.**

Google has made this easy by automatically putting your reply first. If you click on the three little arrows under your message but above the button marked **Send**, then you can see the rest of the email thread will appear below your message.

If you clicked on **Reply** but you actually wanted **Forward**, you can rectify this easily by clicking on the little downwards pointing arrow by the bigger arrow (pointing left) next to the profile picture as seen circled in *figure 5.5*. You can also edit the subject here but bear in mind that when you change the subject, your message will not only appear as a new thread to your recipient but also in your sent emails (which might be confusing if you are looking for it later).

If you click on **Pop out reply** (last in the options shown in figure 5.6), you will be able to type in your message above your other emails in a pop up. This will mean you can flip and refer to other emails while writing your message.

Once you have clicked on **Send**, you will get a message at the top of the screen, highlighted in yellow, to tell you it has been sent.

FIGURE 5.5 Where to find **Forward**.

05

Did you know...

You can have your friend's profile pictures next to their emails if you add them to your contacts.

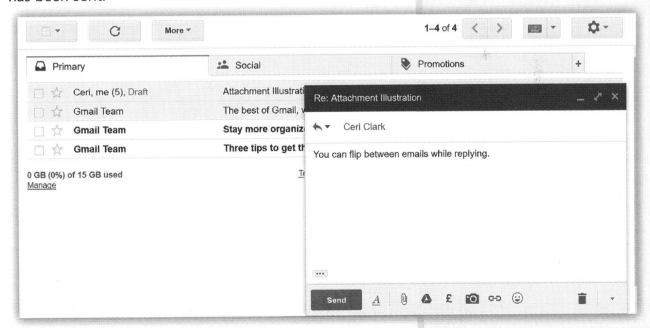

FIGURE 5.6 Using **pop out reply** means you can flip between emails.

Forwarding uses the same method as replying but you will have to put in the email address of the person you want it to go to.

Did you know...

If you want to reply or forward a particular message rather than the whole thread, open the message from the thread and click the Reply button on that particular message. You can choose not to include the quoted text.

FIGURE 5.7 Click the x to remove email addresses

FIGURE 5.8 Where to find Compose.

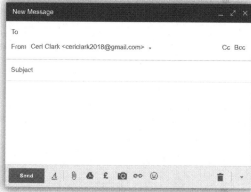

FIGURE 5.9 Compose box.

The options for formatting an email will appear in the *Composing an email* section below.

Replying to a group

If an email has been sent to more than one person in the **To** or **CC** part of an email, then you will have the option to **Reply to all**. Don't do this unless you really want everyone to see your message. The only way to stop the email going to everyone is if you just click on **Reply** and manually add people's email address or when you click on **Reply to all**, you have to delete the people you don't want to see your message manually from the email. You can do this by pressing on the **X** to the right of each person's name (please see *figure 5.7*).

Composing an email

Composing an email is a simple process. In the first column of the page, click on the box labelled **Compose**. See *figure 5.8* for what it looks like.

The compose page will load as a pop up on top of your other messages, ready for you to fill in (please see *figure 5.9*).

Clicking on the **To** will bring up your address book but I am assuming you don't have one yet. If you know the email address, just type it into the white box. If you do have your contacts set up, you can start typing your contact's name and Gmail will give you suggestions as you type. Click on the one that you are looking for. This saves you time and means you don't need to memorise their email address, you just need to know their name.

Type in a descriptive subject and what you want to say in the large box. When you are ready click **Send**. If you have more than one email address setup in Gmail (for example if you own a website domain), you can choose which email address to send from.

Formatting your email

You might think your email is a little boring without formatting. As in a lot of word processors you can change the way an email looks and feels by highlighting what you want changed and clicking the **B** for Bold

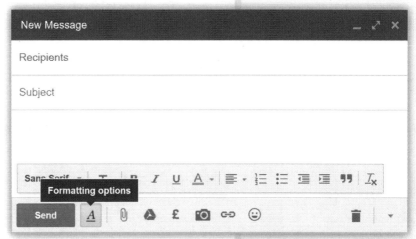

05

FIGURE 5.10 Formatting options.

button, **I** for italics etc. These used to be lined up above the text box but now you have to click on the **A** with a red arrow underneath to see the formatting options.

The formatting options are very like those in any standard word processor. If you are familiar with one of these then you will know how to use them.

Figure 5.11 shows what the buttons look like:

- ***Sans Serif*** – clicking on this will allow you to change font (Sans Serif is the name of a font)
- ***Two Ts*** – Clicking on this button will make your text bigger or smaller
- ***B*** – Bold your text
- ***I*** – Italicize your text
- ***U*** underlined – Underline your text
- ***A*** underlined – Change the color of your text
- ***Six horizontal lines*** – How do you want your paragraphs aligned/ justified?
- ***Horizontal lines with numbers*** – Bullet your text with numbers
- ***Horizontal lines with dots*** – Bullet your text with circles (like this list)
- ***Horizontal lines with an arrow pointing left*** – Indent

Did you know…

Beside the text formatting options you should see a paper clip to add an attachment, a triangle for saving to Drive, a currency symbol to send and request money from Google Wallet, a camera or picture icon to represent adding an image to your email (once you click on this, the instructions are the same as for adding a profile photo), a link for adding hyperlinks and finally a smiley face to add smileys.

FIGURE 5.11 A closer look at the formatting options.

FIGURE 5.12 Link icon.

your text to the left

- ***Horizontal lines with arrow pointing right*** – Indent your text to the right
- ***Quotation mark*** – Quote the text
- ***Underlined T with cross*** – Remove formatting

Adding a link to your email

You may find you want to link to an item at your favorite store for a present or to an article you think your friend might find particularly interesting.

Edit Link

Text to display: Buy this awesome book!

Link to:

To what URL should this link go?

⦿ **Web address** http://anystore.com

○ Email address Test this link

Not sure what to put in the box? First, find the page on the web that you want to link to. (A search engine might be useful.) Then, copy the web address from the box in your browser's address bar, and paste it into the box above.

OK   Cancel

FIGURE 5.13 Choose to add a link to a website or an email address when adding the link.

To add a link to the main body of text, first highlight some text that you would like your email recipient to click on. Next, click on the little picture that looks like a chain (*figure 5.12*) in the row beginning with the **Send** button (as seen in *figure 5.11*). Fill in the **Text to display** (this will already be filled in with the text you highlighted but you can change this here) and **To what URL should this link go?** box and click on **OK**.

When you click on the link button, you can also choose to add a link to an email address, in which case Google will ask for the email address when the button is clicked.

Spell check

Default to full-screen

Label   ▶

Plain text mode

Print

Check spelling

🗑 ⌄

FIGURE 5.14 The spell check can be found next to the trash (bin) symbol at the bottom right of the compose window.

Spell Check is an amazing tool which Google provides for free. To take advantage of this feature click on the little arrow located in the bottom right corner or the pop up box (as seen highlighted in *figure 5.14*).

Once clicked, the spelling mistakes will be highlighted in yellow as shown in figure *5.15*.

To see Google's suggestions and correct the spelling mistakes, click on the highlighted text. Once a misspelt

68

word is clicked, a list of options appears. Select which one you think is right and click on it. The word will be replaced and the yellow highlighting will disappear. You can click on Recheck

by clicking on the little arrow at the bottom right of the compose box.

Don't rely completely on spell check. Notice that it didn't pick up on 'yer' instead of 'you'? There is no substitute for giving your messages a quick read before you send them. Reading them out loud can be especially useful for picking up mistakes.

Another problem you might have noticed is that Google's spell check doesn't like my name. You can fix this by adding names you send to regularly (or even your own) to a custom dictionary. This can only be done on the Chrome browser.

Right-click on your name and choose **Add to dictionary**, Another way to do this is to go to:

chrome://settings/editDictionary

...from your Chrome browser and to add (or delete) names or words there. Theoretically this should work but I have to admit, even though Ceri is in my custom dictionary, Google still does not like it. However, I have found that if you right-click on the highlighted word that Google spell checks for you and click **Ignore**, it does work. If the **Add to dictionary** doesn't work, try **Ignore** instead.

FIGURE 5.15 Google will highlight mistakes in yellow.

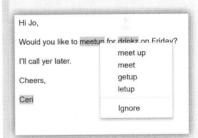

FIGURE 5.16 Select one of Google's suggestions to replace it.

05

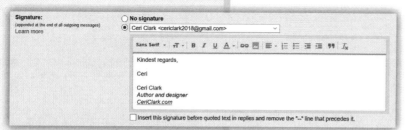

FIGURE 5.17 Adding a signature.

FIGURE 5.18 Add image button.

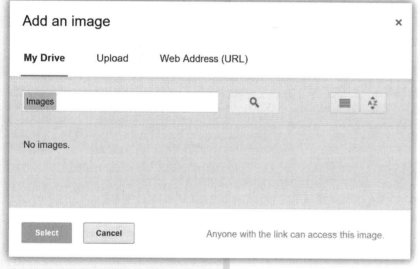

FIGURE 5.19 Options for adding images.

Adding a signature to your emails

A signature can add a personal touch to your emails. It can be used to market your services if you have a business or even just finish off an email if you use the same ending all the time.

You will need to add a signature before you compose your email. This needs to be done in the settings.

First go to the **Gear Wheel** > **Settings** > **General**

Go down the list until you see **Signature**. If you just want a basic signature, you can start typing and formatting what it looks like using the formatting bar directly above the text box.

Check the box before **Insert this signature before quoted text in replies and remove the "--" line that precedes it** to always have your signature in emails you send out.

If you would like to add a photo to your signature, here are the steps you can follow:

1. Click into the text box where you would like the photo to appear
2. Click on the Insert image button

From here, there are three ways to add your images. The first is you search through Google Drive, the second you can upload an image from your computer and the third option is to use a picture from the internet. If you do use an image from the internet please make sure you have the rights to do that. Any public domain image is fine but most images on the internet are copyrighted.

If you choose **Drive**, you can search your images within the search box or browse folders and files that you have in your account. Remember to **Save changes** at the bottom of the settings page when you are happy with your signature.

If you do not have anything suitable in your Google account, then you can search your computer by selecting **Upload** at the top of the pop up as can be seen in *figure 5.19*.

Click on **Select a file** from your computer and search for the picture you want to add. Click on **Open**. Your picture will appear in the signature box. If your picture is too big, click on it and choose one of the options that appear.

You can choose four sizes, small, medium and large, original size or remove the image altogether. Choose **Save changes** at the bottom of the page when you are happy with your signature.

If you want to find an image from the internet, right click on the picture and copy the address. Paste into the box that loads when you click on **Web Address (URL)** when you are choosing how you want to add a picture (*figure 5.21*). Remember to click **Save changes** or the signature won't save.

If you have more than one email linked to your Gmail account then you can have a signature for each email address. Click on the email address that is shown in the email signature section to see the list of addresses drop down so you can select the one you want.

Deleting emails

Look for the trash can/bin symbol to delete emails. You can select more than one email at a time from the Gmail homepage by checking the boxes and choosing the trash symbol at the top of the window.

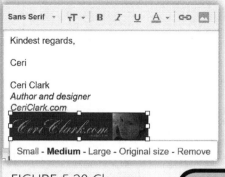

FIGURE 5.20 Change the size of the picture with a click of a button.

05

FIGURE 5.21 Discard draft button in the compose window.

Did you know...

If you receive unwanted email that you never asked for you can report it as spam or phishing to remove it from your Inbox.

For detailed instructions on how to recognise and deal with scams, spam and phishing attacks, take a look at the **Security** chapter near the beginning of this book.

Deleting draft emails

To delete messages before they are sent click on the little trash symbol at the bottom right of the window.

Deleting emails sent to you

To delete emails that are sent to you, first go to the message list on the Gmail homepage by clicking on the Gmail logo, then click on the little box to the left of each email that you want to delete. This adds a tick to the box, and then click on the trash can icon which will appear above your emails list.

Bulk Delete emails

If you would like to delete all emails sent from one address, you can do this by using the '**filter messages like these**' option.

1. First click on the box next to an email which was sent from the address you want to remove
2. Locate **More** at the top of the window and click on it
3. Select **Filter messages like these**
4. Click the **X** at the top of filter pane
5. Manually check the boxes next to the emails and click on the trash can/bin symbol or check the box in the menu above the boxes next to the emails and press the trash can/bin symbol

This is the quickest way to delete a ton of email.

Chapter summary

This chapter covered how to send, receive, format, and delete emails. If you are looking to add links, make your text bold or be in italics or even if you just want to spell check what you have written, you will find that in this chapter. A section on your signature explains how to add, format and add pictures to them.

Chapter 06

Your Contacts (Address Book)

What to expect in this chapter:

- How to get to Google Contacts
- An overview of the homepage
- How to add and edit contacts
- Deleting contacts
- Restoring contacts
- Organizing your contacts using labels and starring
- Importing and exporting your contacts
- Printing your contacts
- Google Contacts settings

Keeping all your contacts online is a great idea. As well as saving on paper, it also means that you can update your contacts wherever you are, whether at home or on a mobile device when travelling. It is all about convenience. Not only does Contacts keep your friends, acquaintances, business and co-worker details in one place it also integrates with your Android phone so that you can call your friend with a touch of a button.

How to get to Google Contacts

There are three ways to get to Google Contacts.

Google Contacts from Gmail

To get to the contacts page from Gmail, click on **Gmail** then, in the drop down menu that appears, (under **Gmail,** but above **Compose) click on Gmail again,** (as seen in *figure 6.1*).

Google Contacts direct address

You can also go directly to your contacts by typing in the following address into the address bar at the top of your browser window:

https://contacts.google.com/

Google Contacts from the Waffle/app launcher

Click on the waffle (the square consisting of squares located on the top right of any Google service you are logged into. Choose Google Contacts from the list that drops down.

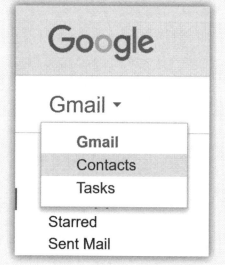

FIGURE 6.1 The location of Contacts in Gmail.

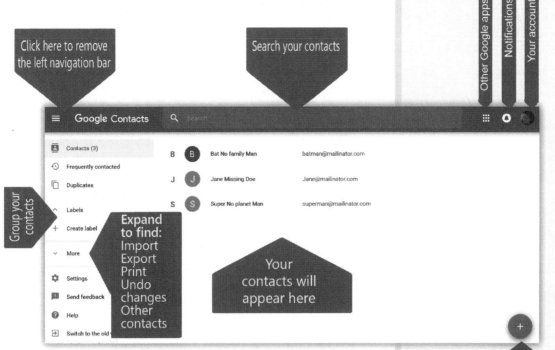

Click here to remove the left navigation bar

Search your contacts

Other Google apps

Notifications

Your account

Group your contacts

Expand to find:
Import
Export
Print
Undo changes
Other contacts

Your contacts will appear here

Add a contact here

Contacts overview

FIGURE 6.2 Google Contacts overview.

Google contacts is effectively another Google service but which is integrated to Gmail. As such it works similarly to Gmail but looks a little different. This section aims to give you a quick overview of the Contacts homepage.

Top navigation bar

The top navigation bar has a menu button (three vertical lines) which will 'collapse' the side navigation. The second item is the search bar which enables you to search within your contacts. You can go to any other Google service, including Gmail, Calendar etc. from the square consisting of 9 smaller squares (otherwise known as a waffle or app launcher). The notifications are Google+ and Google Photos, and the final item in the top navigation bar is your profile picture. This allows you to get to your Google Account settings which includes privacy, security and account preferences.

Left navigation pane

You will mostly be using the left navigation pane to get around Google Contacts along with the little red circle with the plus sign in it.

- **Contacts**: Clicking on this will bring up all your contacts

- **Frequently contacted**: This will show you the people you email the most

- **Duplicates**: Google will put any duplicates it finds on this page. You can then choose to merge them if you wish

- **Labels**: This is how you group your contacts into categories. Click on **Create label** to add groups such as work, family, friends etc.

- **More**: Select this to get more options which are **Import**, **Export**, **Print**, **Undo changes**, and **Other contacts**

- **Settings**: You can choose your Google-wide language here.. This means that what you set here will take effect in Gmail, Docs and other services. You can also sort your contacts here by first name, last name

- **Help**: Click here to get to Google's help pages

- **Switch to the old version**: You can go back to the old Google contacts view by clicking here but it is not recommended. This version will become permanent eventually and there is no point in learning another way of using Google contacts in the interim

Contacts pane

All your contacts will appear here in a list determined by what you choose in **Settings** in the left navigation pane. They will appear in alphabetical order. Any starred contacts will appear at the top of the list.

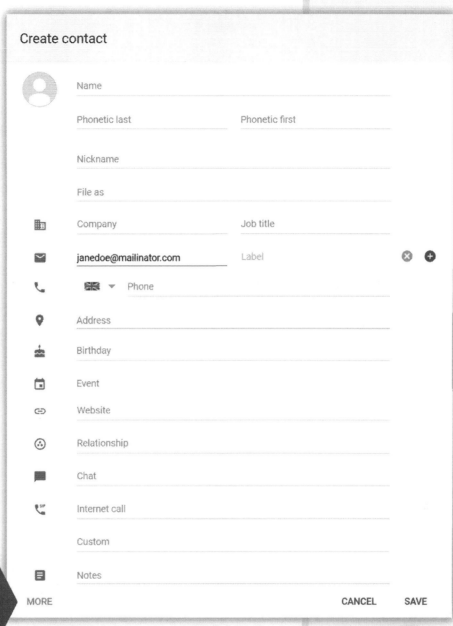

Create contact

Name

Phonetic last | Phonetic first

Nickname

File as

Company | Job title

janedoe@mailinator.com | Label

Phone

Address

Birthday

Event

Website

Relationship

Chat

Internet call

Custom

Notes

MORE | CANCEL | SAVE

Click MORE to get the complete set of options

Click on the red button with the plus to bring up the Create contact form.

Add contacts

The red circle with the plus symbol is the place to add new contacts to the service.

FIGURE 6.3 Click on the add a contact button and More to get all the options.

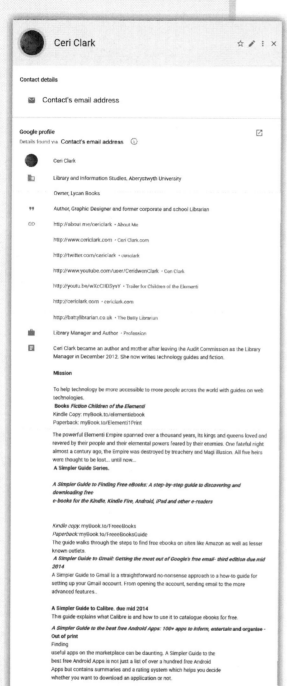

FIGURE 6.4 My contact details filled in when you put in my personal email address.

How to add contacts using the Gmail website

Once the page has loaded click on the red circle with the white plus (as seen in *figure 6.3)* on the bottom right of the screen.

Adding a contact using an email address

If you know the email address of your contact and they have a public profile with Google, you can automatically add a profile picture and some personal information just by clicking into the email field and adding the email address then **SAVE**.

Figure 6.4 shows my details filled into a contact just by adding my personal email address.

This information is purely from Google. You will still need to fill in details like name, address and phone number etc. for example, as most people will keep these details private. This information is not editable and you cannot remove it. It is at the bottom of the details though under the heading Google profile so you can avoid it by not scrolling that far in the record!

Please bear in mind, because you do not have control over this information, it could be out of date depending on how much of a Google+ user your contact is. I have to confess the information in My Google+ profile is about 5 years out of date. The contact details are correct but I haven't been a Library Manager since 2013!

Select the contact name on the Google Contacts homepage and click on the little pen symbol (see *figure 6.4)* on the top right of the screen. These symbols also appear when you hover over your contact's names as well.

You won't see the place to add the address until you click

on **More.** This can be seen on the bottom left of *figure 6.3*).

Simply type in the boxes (or into the next one) to put in the details. Remember to click **SAVE** once you have finished.

Filling in the fields

There are a small number of options when you first click on the **add address** button (red circle with plus). You will not be able to add an address until you click on **More.**

- Name
- Company
- Job Title
- Email
- Phone
- Notes

When you click on More on the left, these extra options appear:

- Phonetic last, phonetic first
- Nickname
- File as
- Address
- Birthday
- Event
- Website
- Relationship
- Chat
- Internet Call
- Custom

The explanations below cover the options in the order as they appear when you click More.

06

FIGURE 6.5 Company icon in Google Contacts.

Name, Company, Phonetic First, Phonetic Last and Nickname

These are mostly self-explanatory. The phonetic first and last name options are for names you are unfamiliar with. For example my name is Ceri but you could type it in the **Phonetic first** field as Kerry. This would remind you how my name is pronounced should we ever meet. Android also uses the phonetic name to aid in voice recognition.

The nickname is just the non-formal name you call your contact. In the name you could have Elizabeth Taylor. In the Nickname you could have Lizzie, In the search box, you could search for any of these three things and her information would load.

The full contact name takes priority when you are emailing or when you are looking for someone on your phone. However, typing names in the **Nickname** and **File as** boxes means you can search for these variants and find them easier.

File as is another way to label your contacts. It does not appear in your email or the auto-complete when you start typing in a name in the **To** field when composing an email. What it does do is change how your contacts are listed in Google Contacts itself. For example, if your mother's name is Joan Rivers but you put in *Mother* in the **File as** box then in Google Contacts, she will appear as *Mother*. However, when you type *Mother* in the **To** field, Gmail will not be able to find her and you will have to type in Joan to find her. The only way around this is if you put *Mother - Joan Rivers* or *Joan Rivers - Mother* as the contact name.

Email, Phone and Address

The Email, Phone and Address can all be customized. Type in your friend's email address, and click **DONE** or continue to fill in the fields. (If you know the email address of your contact and they have a public Google profile, all their public details will be filled in by default). If you click on **DONE** straight after you have typed in the email address, you will see a profile photo is added and other information

FIGURE 6.6 Email icon in Google Contacts.

FIGURE 6.7 Phone icon in Google Contacts.

FIGURE 6.8 Address icon in Google Contacts.

from your contact's Google+ profile. It will be populated with all the information they have made public in their Google+ profile. Once this is done, you can go back and fill in the information that is missing.

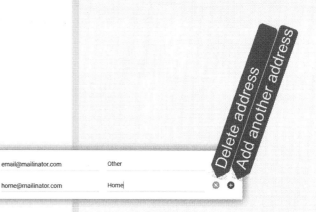

You can choose to assign the home, work or other label to the email address. This is for informational use and not for organising. It does not show up under Labels on the navigation panel. This is useful when your contact has a number of email addresses and you want to instantly see which email address applies to what area of their life. If your friend is on holiday, there is no point emailing their work address for example. They may have a work email address, a home address, a club address and so on.

FIGURE 6.9 Add or delete email addresses in the contact's details.

You can keep on adding email addresses by clicking on the plus that appears at the end of the email address row. Please see *figure 6.9* for where this is located. You can also delete email addresses by clicking on the **x** next to the plus.

Phone numbers and addresses are similar. Follow the same steps as above to customize these fields. You could also use the phone labels to call someone. For example, tell your phone "call Jane home" and it will call Jane on her home phone number.

FIGURE 6.10 Birthday icon in Google Contacts.

Birthday and Event

Under **Address** there is the option of putting your contact's birthday in. Type in the format 05/14/1960 in the United States or 14/05/1960 in the United Kingdom. Make sure that your language settings are correct for your region or Google will interpret the date incorrectly. You can just type anything in here however and it will work. 3rd May 2010 will work but if you type in 03/05/2010 Google will interpret it as March or May depending on where Google thinks you are.

FIGURE 6.11 Events icon in Google Contacts.

Google gives you the option of adding events. This can be labelled anniversary or any other special date by typing in

81

FIGURE 6.12 Website icon in Google Contacts.

FIGURE 6.13 Relationship icon in Google Contacts.

FIGURE 6.14 Chat icon in Google Contacts.

a date and choosing a label they suggest or typing your own in the label box. As with the other details you can delete them or add more events by clicking on the **x** and **plus** icons.

Website

If your contact has a website, put the address next to **website**. You can add as many websites as you like using the plus icon. Press the **x** if you want to delete them. Google suggests you label the websites Profile, Blog, Homepage or Work but you can just type anything into the field and it will work. If this contact relates to work, this could be your contact's company website.

Relationship

The relationship section of your contact's details is important if you want to use voice to call them on your Android phone. If you put any relationship in, you can then ask Google to call or text them using your Nickname without touching your phone. It does not matter what you put in the relationship. I typed in 'better half' just to see if it worked and it did. The important information is the nickname but you can literally put anything in the relationship space as long as there is something there.

1. Next to relationship type in your relationship to your contact
2. Make sure the Nickname is what you want to tell your phone. Think about how it might sound if you are in public talking to Google
3. Say "OK Google" to your phone
4. Say "Text nickname", or "Call nickname"

Google will ask you to confirm the contact and will then do as you ask.

Chat

Type in your contact's chat ID next to Chat. Google suggests that you can label them Google Talk, AIM, Yahoo,

Skype, QQ, MSN, ICQ and Jabber. Use the + and x to add and delete Chat IDs.

Internet call

Type in your internet call information in here and label it Home, Work or Other.

06

FIGURE 6.15 Internet call icon in Google Contacts.

Custom

Like the **Notes** information, you can put anything you like in here. The only difference is that you can label the information to make it easier to find and understand.

Notes

Last but not least there is a big box with **Add a note** to the right. This is invaluable for work or acquaintances. Add as much or as little information as you want here. This could be particularly useful if you can't remember when or where you met someone.

FIGURE 6.16 Notes icon in Google Contacts.

Adding photos to Contacts

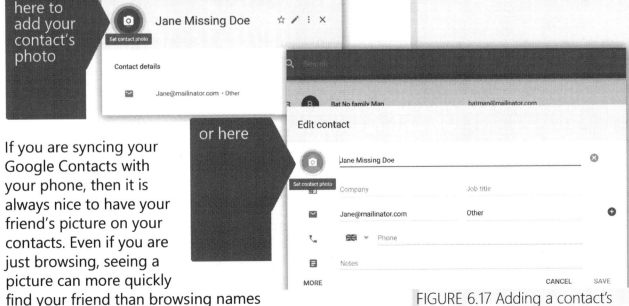

Click here to add your contact's photo

If you are syncing your Google Contacts with your phone, then it is always nice to have your friend's picture on your contacts. Even if you are just browsing, seeing a picture can more quickly find your friend than browsing names down a list.

FIGURE 6.17 Adding a contact's photo.

FIGURE 6.18 Upload photos or access your photos in your Google account.

FIGURE 6.19 On an existing contact, click the pen/pencil icon to edit your contact.

By clicking on **Set contact photo**, a pop up will appear asking you to browse your computer for a suitable picture. Remember to click **Save** when you are done.

Browse your computer or click on the photos that Google finds in your account across its services. You will be given the opportunity to edit your picture before you click done. Use the round arrows at the top to rotate the image or left-click on the image and drag down or up to resize it. When you are happy click on **DONE**. The picture will be turned into a circle.

If you want to change the picture later, click on the existing image and choose another or click on **Remove photo**.

Editing Contacts

To change the details on your contacts, click on your contacts name and choose the pencil/pen icon as seen in *figure 6.19*.

Deleting Contacts

There are two easy methods for deleting contacts. Method 1 is best for deleting one contact and the second method is great for deleting multiple contacts at the same time.

Method 1: Deleting one contact

1. Click on the contact you want to delete
2. Click on the three vertical dots
3. Select **delete**
4. Confirm you want to remove the contact(s) by clicking on **DELETE** again

Method 2: Deleting multiple contacts

1. Click on the profile photo or big letter in a circle next to the name of the contact(s) you want to delete

2. Click on the three vertical dots as circled in *figure 6.20*

3. Click on the trash can (bin) icon or the word **Delete**

4. Confirm you want to remove the contact(s) by clicking on **DELETE** again

You can hide contacts by following the same steps but choosing **hide** instead of delete at the end.

FIGURE 6.20 Deleting multiple contacts.

Restoring contacts (Undo changes)

If you have accidentally removed your contacts and you want them back there is a way to get them back by restoring them to a previous time.

1. Click on **More** in the left navigation pane

2. Click on **Undo changes**

3. Choose how far back in time you want to reset your Google Contacts to

4. Click on **CONFIRM**

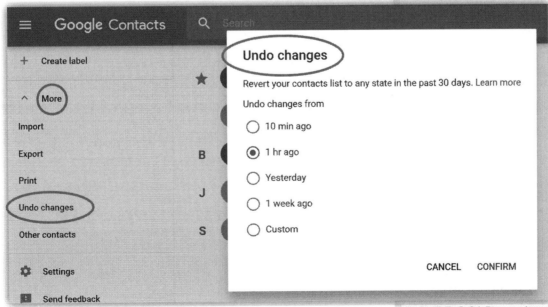

FIGURE 6.21 Restoring your contacts.

Did you know...

You can have your contacts in more than one label. For example your best friend may work for a certain company and so you might want your friend in your Friends label but also in the Anycompany PLC label.

If you chose *Yesterday*, your contacts list and details will revert back to how they were the day before and so on for week etc.

Starring your contacts

You can star your contacts to make them easier to find. When you star a contact it will go to the top of the list. Select your contact and then click on the star icon. It appears next to the pencil symbol as seen in *figure 6.19*.

Grouping your contacts using Labels

With labels you can organize all your contacts into groups. Why should you add labels? If you have hundreds of contacts in a long list, it can be time consuming to find the name you need. Of course you can search for them, but what if you can't remember how to spell their name or even what their name is?

You may for example have a label for Anycompany PLC. You know you want to talk to the director's PA but can't remember her name. With two thousand contacts (you are very popular), it would be impossible to find him/her just from browsing.

This is where **Labels** comes into its own. When you were putting your contacts from Anycompany PLC into your contacts you created a label of the same name. Now when you go in to your contacts, your groups of people (labels) will appear on the left in the **Labels** section. You just click on Anycompany PLC and a list of contacts at that company will appear in the main window.

Of course you could also search for PA in the search window as long as you put his/her job title in their details.

How to add a label

First either click on **Create label** in the left navigation bar

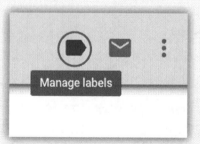

FIGURE 6.22 Manage labels button.

or click on a profile photo and then **Manage labels** symbol/icon and click on **Create label** as illustrated in the next graphic. You will not be able to create a new label from the contact page itself only add existing labels. You will need to create a new label from the left navigation bar or from the top of the page when you click in the box that appears when you click on a profile photo.

FIGURE 6.23 Managing labels from the contact's page.

Adding labels from the Google Contact's homepage

1. Click on **Create label** in the left navigation bar
2. Type in your group name and click **OK**
3. Click on your contact's profile pictures or the circles with their first initial in it
4. Look to the top of your browser window and select the **Manage labels** button (to see what this looks like, please see *figure 6.22*
5. Choose from the labels you have already made from the dropdown list or select **Create label** to make another one

Adding Labels from a contact's page

1. Go into your contact by clicking on to their name
2. Click on the three horizontal dots (see *figure 6.23* for the circled location)
3. Choose one or more existing labels by selecting them

If you want to check that the right groups have been assigned, go into your contact's page and then look under their name. They will be listed in alphabetical order as seen in *figure 6.24*.

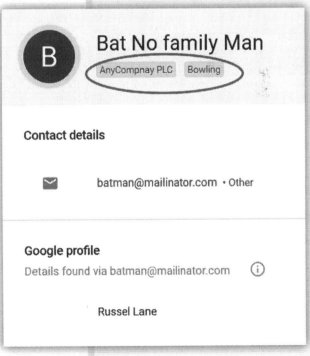

FIGURE 6.24 The labels assigned will show under your contact's name.

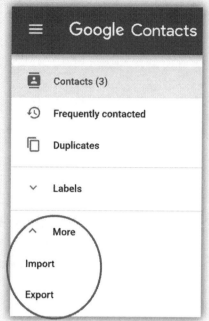

FIGURE 6.25 Location of Import and export options.

Importing and exporting contacts

You may want to either import contacts from another source or export them to share them with colleagues, friends or family. Google makes this easy, please follow the next steps to add or share your contacts.

Importing Contacts

If someone has sent you a vCard or a spreadsheet with contacts and you want to import it or you want to import your contacts from another email address, Google has made this really easy to do. The services they support are Yahoo Mail, Outlook.com, AOL, other email providers and of course a CSV or vCard. Here are some quick instructions on how to do it.

Importing from another email service

FIGURE 6.26 Import from a CSV, vCard or another internet service.

The act of importing from another email service is done by a third party service, which at the time of writing was ShuttleCloud. You will need to agree to their terms of service and privacy policy to proceed. It is better to use a CSV or vCard file as you won't be giving someone else access to your other email account.

However, if you want to import information using this method, here are the steps to follow.

1. From the Google Contacts homepage (in the left navigation bar), click on **More**
2. Next click on **Import**. A pop up will appear with several options
3. Select you email provider in the list Google offers. If you cannot see yours, choose **Other email provider**
4. Click on **AGREE, LET'S GO!**
5. Follow the on-screen instructions. You will need to login to your other email account so they know it

is you that is trying to access the account and not someone else

Importing from a CSV or vCard file

A vCard or CSV file is a spreadsheet that can be read by different spreadsheet programs such as Google Sheets or Microsoft Excel. You can back this up on your computer or even send them to your friends. If there is anything on there that you do not want your friend to see, edit it in a spreadsheet, save it and then send it to them.

1. From the Google Contacts homepage (in the left navigation bar), click on **More**

2. Next click on **Import**. A pop up will appear with several options

3. Select **CSV or vCard file**

4. At the time of writing, Importing is only available in the old view of Google contacts. Click on **GO TO OLD VERSION** in the pop up box

5. Go to the **More** menu (under the search bar) and click on **Import**

6. Click on **Browse** and search for the file in your computer

7. Lastly, click on Import and Google will add the contacts in the CSV or vCard file into your contacts

8. Go back to the new version of Google Contacts by clicking on **Try Contacts preview** at the bottom of the left navigation bar

9. Refresh your browser

Exporting Contacts

If you would like to export your contacts you can do this with a vCard or via CSV which is a spreadsheet that can be read by different spreadsheet programs such as Google Sheets or Microsoft Excel. As with importing contacts at the time of writing, Google hasn't enabled the function for the new view of Google Contacts. You will need to revert to the old version and then back to the new when you are finished.

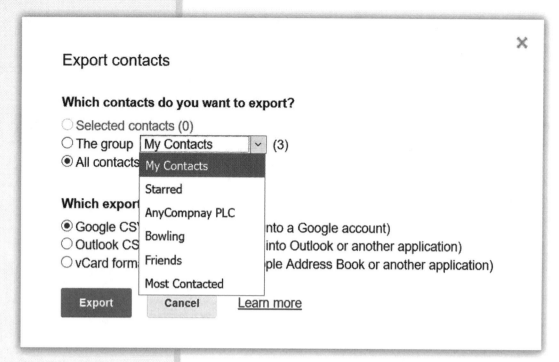

Export contacts   ✕

Which contacts do you want to export?

○ Selected contacts (0)
○ The group | My Contacts ▾ | (3)
◉ All contacts | My Contacts |

          Starred

Which export   AnyCompnay PLC

◉ Google CSV   Bowling   nto a Google account)
○ Outlook CS   into Outlook or another application)
○ vCard form Friends   ple Address Book or another application)

          Most Contacted

   Export   Cancel   Learn more

FIGURE 6.27 Export contact options.

1. Click on **More** in the left navigation bar
2. Click on **Export**
3. Click on **GO TO OLD VERSION**
4. Click on **More** in the navigation bar (below the search bar at the top of the browser)
5. Click on **Export**. A pop-up will load with three options for which contacts you want to export and three options for what type of file you want to export it as

You can preselect one of your contacts before starting the export process for the first option (as illustrated in the figure above). This allows you to just export that contact.

The second choice asks if you want to export all your contacts in a group/label and the third will export all your contacts. You can obviously only select one of the top three options at a time.

The second set of options asks you how you want it to be exported. The type of CSV (a type of spreadsheet) that will work with another Google account will be different from a Microsoft Outlook or another application, so you must choose the option for where you want to export to. The third option is a vCard which can be imported into Apple Address books as well as some other applications.

Did you know...

Back up your contacts by exporting them all to a CSV file and saving them on your computer.

In the unlikely event that the **Undo changes** option doesn't work and if you have any problems with your Google Contacts in the future, just delete what is in there and import them again!

90

6. Click on **Export** and save the file to your computer. The suggested file name is google.csv but you can change this if you want to

7. Go back to the new version of Google Contacts by clicking on **Try Contacts preview** at the bottom of the left navigation bar

8. Refresh your browser

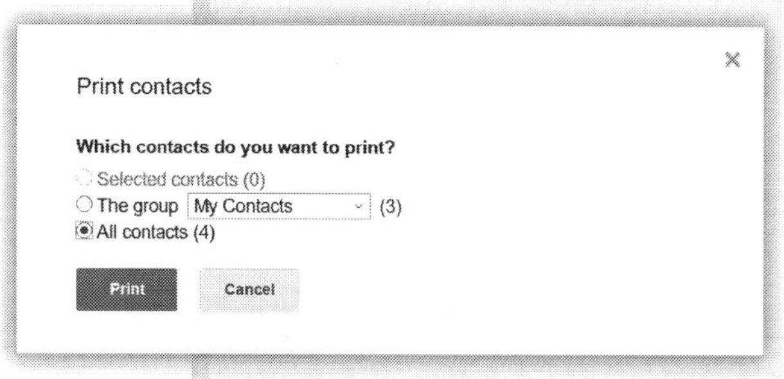

FIGURE 6.28 Printing options.

Printing your contacts list

Again you will need to go back to the old version to print out your contacts. Everything should stay the same when it is implemented within the new Contacts view but the look will probably change. For now, the instructions for printing out your contacts are as follows:

1. Click on **More** in the left navigation bar

2. Click on **Print**

3. Click on **GO TO OLD VERSION**

4. Click on **More** in the navigation bar (below the search bar at the top of the browser)

5. Click on **Print**

6. Make your choice and click on **Print**. A new page will load with your contents displayed in a list

7. In Windows click on **Ctrl** while tapping the **P** button to bring up the print dialog box. You can choose to save it as a PDF or send to your printer. On an Apple computer, press on **Command** and tap on **P** for your print options

8. Go back to the new version of Google Contacts by clicking on **Try Contacts preview** at the bottom of the left navigation bar

FIGURE 6.29 What the list will look like when you click **PRINT.**

9. Refresh your browser

Other Contacts

On the left navigation bar, under **More**, you will see an option for **Other contacts**. These are contacts you didn't add but are found within your Google account. These could be people that emailed you or people that you added in Google+.

If you have contacts that you know have emailed you but you haven't added to Google Contacts, you can add them from the contact's page.

Ceri Clark
Add to contacts
Contact details

FIGURE 6.30 Click on **Add to contacts** to add them to your main contacts list.

1. Click on your contact's name from the Google Contacts home-page
2. Click on the **Add to contacts** button. It looks like a + beside a person icon. Please see *figure 6.30* for how this looks

That's it. If you close the pop up and click on Google Contacts on the top of your screen, the contact will now appear in your list of contacts on the homepage.

Google Contacts settings

Settings
Language
Change your language setting for all Google products
Phone number country code
United Kingdom
Sort by
First name
Last name
CANCEL
SAVE

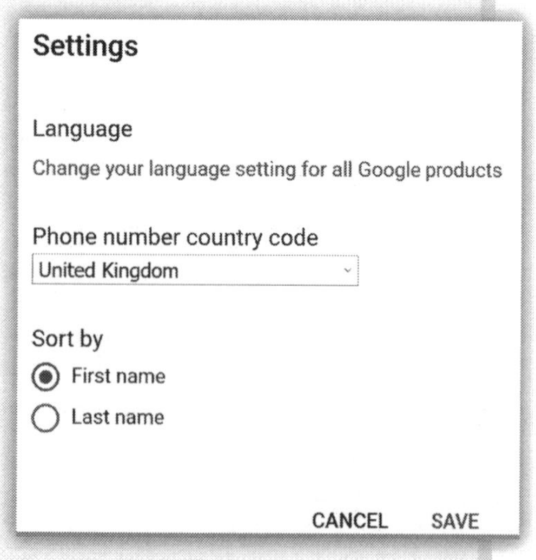

FIGURE 6.31 Google contacts settings.

The settings for Google Contacts are basic but it is worth reviewing them as they can have a big impact on how you use it.

The link to get to the settings on the Google Contacts service is located on the bottom of the left navigation bar.

Language

If you change your language here, it will affect Gmail and all the other Google services that you use, including Google Docs etc. This will affect your spell check.

Phone number country code

Add the country where you live to this section.

Sort by

You can choose to sort your contacts on the homepage by their first name or last name. The **Name** section in your contact's details takes precedence, unless you choose **File as** which will supersede the name you input.

Duplicate contacts

If you have duplicate contacts within Google Contacts you can merge them into one contact using **Duplicates**. Google will not always find your duplicate contacts. If the only information your duplicate records share is their name, then it won't find them. However, if two or more records share the same email address or phone number then you should be able to find it by clicking on **Duplicates** on the left hand side of the browser in Google Contacts.

If Google does find any duplicates they will appear in a box. Click on **MERGE** on the bottom right of the box for all the records to be merged into one.

Chapter summary

Google Contacts is an essential service that is integrated into Gmail. It is where all your friends, co-workers, business and other contact details are held. This chapter explains what is available and how to do some important tasks, including:

- How to get to Google Contacts from Gmail, direct by internet address or from any Google service you are logged into
- A Google contacts homepage overview
- How to add contacts

- Editing contacts
- Deleting one or more contacts
- Restoring your contacts if you accidentally remove them
- Starring your contacts to make them appear at the top of your list
- Grouping your contacts using labels to more easily find your contacts by relationship, work or any other kind of category
- Importing and exporting contacts to and from Google
- How to print your contacts in a list
- Where to find other contacts and how to integrate them into your main list. These could be people who have emailed you but you haven't manually added them to your account. Google allows you to find them in **Other contacts** and add them from there
- What are the settings available in Google Contacts and what do they mean

Chapter 07

Email Organization
with Labels

What to expect in this chapter:

- What are Labels?

- How to create them

- How to customize your labels

- How to apply your labels

- Removing labels

Did you know...

The Inbox is just a label. If you remove the Inbox label (or archive it), you can find the emails again by searching for it or looking in **All Mail**.

Google is second to none as a tool for organizing emails. There are four big guns in the Google arsenal. These are discussions (mentioned in detail in *Chapter 5*), filters (find out more in *chapter 8*), Labels and Spam protection (*Chapter 4 Security*). This chapter will look in depth at labels.

Labels

Labels are what folders were in other programs and that antiquated filing cabinet gathering dust in the corner of your garage (because of course you have a paperless home office now). I used to have folders for everything including folders within folders. I had folders for holidays, work, friends, shopping, advice and many more. The old way was organized but there was always a point where you had to make a choice of where something went in your folder structure. For example if I planned a holiday with my friend to go shopping. Which folder would it go under? I would have chosen holidays in the past. Probably narrowing it down to Holidays > New York or something to that effect.

With Google Mail (Gmail) you don't have to make that choice, create the labels and add them all to the one email. If I look in any of the Holidays, New York, Friends or Shopping labels I can now find it easily and quickly. Simply put, you can label your emails with as many 'labels' as you want. Whatever makes it easier to find the information you need. Labels can be described as categories, folders, groups, tags or just labels.

Creating a Label

Making a label is simple. Click on the **gear symbol** at the top right of the webpage (when you hover your mouse over the gear wheel it should confirm that it is the settings function). A dropdown menu will appear - you will need to select **Settings**. The reason you have to select it twice is that Google has put a few extra cosmetic options which they feel you might need to see first, such as how compact you would like the webpage to appear, and a **configure your inbox** option. Click on **Labels** as in number 1 in

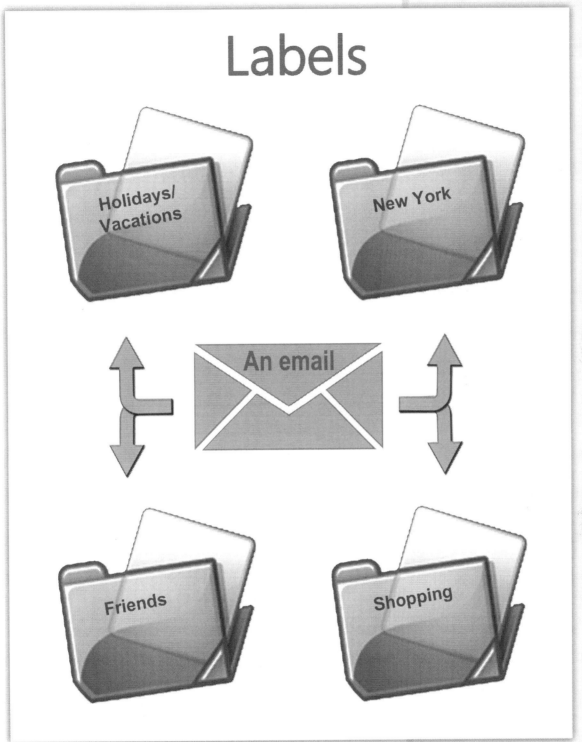

Labels

FIGURE 7.1 **Many labels can be given to one email.**

figure 7.2. Scroll down the page, past **System Labels** and **Categories** until you will see just Labels as in the section labelled number 2 in *figure 7.2*.

Click on **Create new label** as seen in the next figure (the arrow marked 2). Type in the box the label name you want,

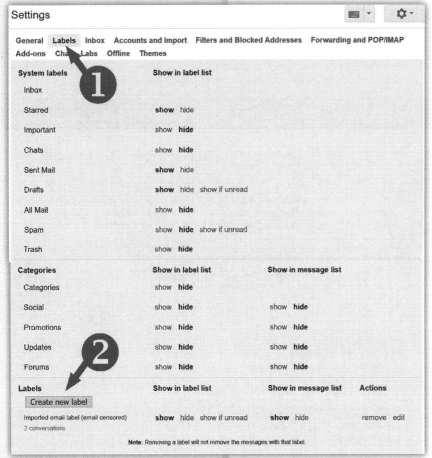

FIGURE 7.2 How to get to the labels section.

for example *Shopping* and think about if you want it to be a nested label.

A nested label means that a label will appear under another in the label list. This will require a little forethought if you want to keep your emails organized. You don't want to keep chopping and changing your labels. It could get confusing!

Nesting labels is similar to the file structure you will find in a computer. You have a main category like for example, *Shopping*, then underneath you could have several other categories like, *groceries, clothes, electronics* etc.

In *figure 7.3* I am creating a new label called **Groceries** which will be nested under **Shopping**.

Later, I will use a filter that will send all my receipt emails from my grocery stores to the **Groceries** label so I don't have to deal with them as they come in but I can find them later.

I want to cut down the number of labels that appear in the Gmail sidebar but still have easy access to the more specific labels. To do this, I have put **Groceries** under **Shopping**. This means I will be able to find it quicker and all similar emails will be in the same place.

The quick steps for doing this are:

FIGURE 7.3 Nested labels.

1. Go to **Settings**
2. Then **Settings** again (in the drop-down list)
3. Click on **Labels**
4. Select **Create New Label**
5. Type your **Label**
6. Select a parent label (to be nested under)
7. Click **Create**

Your new Label will then appear in the list of Labels below the box.

Groceries now appears under **Shopping**. If you click on the little arrow to the left of the Shopping label (as seen circled in *figure 7.4*), you can show or hide the Groceries label and any other label you have 'nested' under Shopping.

I would like to sound a note of warning about the use of nested labels. If you label an email with Groceries, even though it will be under Shopping in the list, the email will not appear if you just click on Shopping. Therefore if you want it to be available under the two labels then you must make sure that both labels are assigned on an email. This way the email will appear when you look under each label.

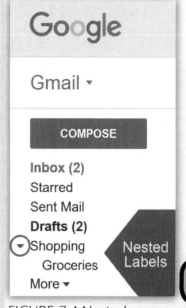

FIGURE 7.4 Nested labels as they will appear in Gmail.

Customizing your labels

All the labels can be customized further. There is a little arrow to the right of each label in the left navigation section on the Gmail homepage. Once you click on this, a menu will appear with more options. Please take a look at *figure 7.5* for the list of options.

A particularly useful feature is that you can change the color of the labels. For example if you have an urgent label, you could color it red. If your favorite color is blue why not make your Friends label blue?

Under the label list, you can show the

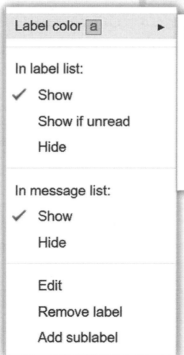

FIGURE 7.5 Click on the arrow to the right of the label that appears when you hover over it to get these options. **Add sublabel** at the bottom of this menu can be a quicker way to make labels.

label, only show it if there are unread emails in it or hide the label entirely from the menu on the left of your Gmail homepage.

FIGURE 7.6 Show or hide the labels in your message list.

There are two options under the message list. This means you can show or hide the label in the row your email appears in the message list on the Gmail homepage. The difference can be seen in *figure 7.6*.

The other options in the submenu are **Edit**, **Remove label** or **Add sublabel**.

Edit your label from the submenu

When you choose **Edit**, you can change the name or add/ remove a parent label. If you remove the parent label and it is the direct 'child' then it will appear alongside the former parent label in the label list on the homepage.

Remove the label from the submenu

Choosing **Remove label** will delete the label but any emails that were categorised under it will still exist. It will not have a label attached (unless you have categorized it under several labels. If this happens, your emails will become 'orphaned' but you can always find emails under **All mail**. To find **All mail** click on **More** directly under your label list on the homepage.

Add sublabel from the submenu

The last option in the list allows you to create a new label. It doesn't matter which label you clicked into to get to this option. The box that will appear will allow you to choose any of your labels to nest under.

Applying a Label

Now that you have created a Label you will want to add it to your email.

From the email list

Check the box on the left of the email that you would like to label. Once you have done this, options for organizing your emails will appear above the email list. Choose the icon (picture) that looks like a luggage label as illustrated in *figure 7.7* by clicking on the little arrow to the right of the icon. A dropdown list will appear.

Tick the box next to the label you want. You can choose as many as you like. If you have too many labels to appear in the list without scrolling you can save time by searching for the labels by typing a few characters in the search box. You don't need to search for the whole word. **Create new** at the bottom of the list will do exactly as the name suggests and will allow you to create a new label. By clicking on **Manage labels** you will be taken to the Labels page in the settings area of Gmail.

From an opened email

The options are similar to applying labels from the list of emails in the Gmail homepage. Choose the luggage tag icon above your emails (see *figure 7.7* to see what this looks like)..

At this point you can assign as many Labels as you want to it. Once you click **Apply**, the email will be assigned or 'moved' to the Label 'folder' or category.

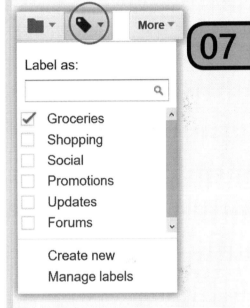

07

FIGURE 7.7 Click the luggage label icon to apply a label.

101

FIGURE 7.8 How to search for all emails from one address.

Google has its own set of labels which it calls categories. These are Social, Promotions, Updates and Forums. These are still labels though and can be found in the labels section of the settings.

Applying a label to more than one email

You can select the boxes next to your emails in the message list and choose the luggage icon, but what if all your emails are not in your message list?

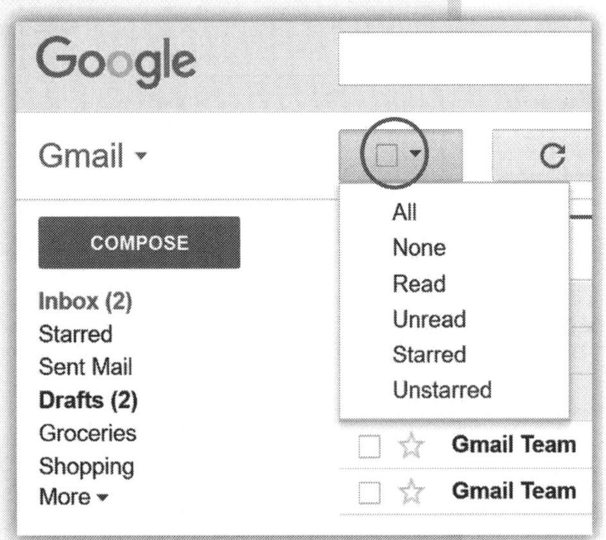

You can label all emails from the same address at the same time using the **Filter messages like these** option. Here is how to do it.

1. Choose an email with the address you want to label

2. Click on More, at the top of your screen

3. Choose **Filter messages like these**

4. Click on the search button at the bottom of the pop-up that loads. All the emails in the list will be from that email address

5. Click on the arrow next to the empty square at the top of your message list

6. Choose **All**

7. If the emails go onto the next page, Gmail will tell you at the top of the page "*All 100 conversations on this page are selected. Select all conversations that match this search*". Click on **Select all conversations that match this search**

8. Click on the luggage tag icon

9. Uncheck the boxes/labels you want to remove. You may have to click more than once to empty the box

10. Click on **Apply**

FIGURE 7.9 Select more than one email quickly.

Removing Labels

You can remove labels easily from emails or several email at once. This section will show you how.

Removing labels from an email

FIGURE 7.10 Click on the **x** to remove the label.

To remove a Label from an email, click on the **x** next to the Label. Your labels can be found next to or below the subject in your emails.

Removing labels from several emails

If you want to remove a label from several emails in your message list, select the email you want to remove the labels from and click on the luggage label button. Uncheck the boxes and click **Apply**.

If the emails you want to remove the label from are in one label, all the emails can be changed at once.

1. Choose the label from the left navigation bar. All the emails will be in that category
2. Click on the arrow next to the empty square at the top of your message list
3. Choose **All**
4. Click on the luggage tag icon
5. Uncheck the boxes/labels you want to remove. You may have to click more than once to empty the box
6. Click on **Apply**

Chapter summary

This chapter is all about labels. It describes how labels are like folders and that more than one label can be assigned to one email. This means you can find an email in more

103

than one place when you are browsing your emails. There are instructions for creating, customizing and applying them, as well as removing labels from one or more emails.

Chapter 08

Filters and Blocked Addresses

What to expect in this chapter:

- What are filters
- Making filters
- Importing filters
- Exporting filters
- Editing filters
- Deleting filters
- Blocked addresses

Applying labels to everything can be a bit of a chore; however Google has come up with an elegant solution with their *Filters* option to save you time.

Filters can allow you to automate the process of adding labels. With this system, if you always want to put all emails from Auntie Flo in a Label called Auntie Flo as soon as they arrive in your inbox without you having to constantly apply labels, then you can get Filters to do this. You can also ask it to treat her emails as very important. It might not mean that you answer her emails any faster but it will mean that you won't lose them amongst the hundreds of other emails you get, or in the spam folder.

Filters also allow you to immediately delete emails from people or companies without ever seeing them or just archive them for later viewing. You can make sure that certain emails never go into spam and that they are marked important or are starred so they are easy to find in the mix of emails you will get daily. Filters are an essential resource for email organization.

Creating a Filter

Go to **Settings** on the top right of the screen (the gear symbol) and choose settings from the dropdown then select **Filters and Blocked Addresses**. Please see steps 1-3

FIGURE 8.1 How to get to Filters

in *figure 8.1*.

Click on **Create a new filter**, (Step 4 in the image above).

The options that Google offer you in Filters can be seen in *figure 8.2*.

Examples of how to filter:

FIGURE 8.2 Filter options

- To label all emails from a person or mailing list, type the email address into the **From** box. For example, *auntieflo@gmail.com*. If you put the email in the **To** box, it will filter all the emails you sent *them*

- If there are specific words in the subject you want to pay attention to, for example if you receive a newsletter from *horse riding weekly* and you want to make sure they all appear together in one place then put *horse riding weekly* into the **Subject** box

- **Has the words** are for general keywords, for example any emails containing a place, name or brand. It is best to use unusual words or you will end up with emails which are not relevant

- The **Doesn't have** is a powerful tool. If you want to label all emails with a word but you are getting too many results and all the wrong results have the same word in them, pop that word into this box and it will ignore those emails with the wrong word in them

- **Has attachment**. If you want all emails with attachments from a certain person to go in the Trash/Bin then, type in the person's name in the **From** box and click the box by **Has attachment** and you will never receive the emails again

Remember you can use one of the filter options or all. You are only limited by your imagination. Once you have put the words you want in the filter, you can choose to search for emails and they will appear in your messages list or you can create a filter.

If you only want to Search, click on the Search button (button with magnifying glass icon) to see if there are

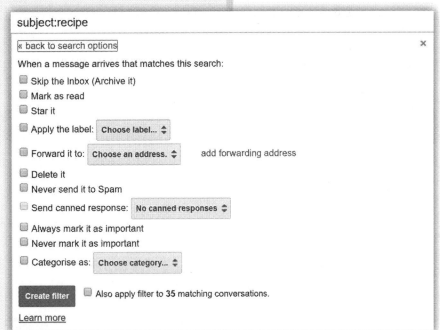

subject:recipe

« back to search options   ×

When a message arrives that matches this search:

☐ Skip the Inbox (Archive it)
☐ Mark as read
☐ Star it
☐ Apply the label: Choose label... ▼
☐ Forward it to: Choose an address. ▼   add forwarding address
☐ Delete it
☐ Never send it to Spam
☐ Send canned response: No canned responses ▼
☐ Always mark it as important
☐ Never mark it as important
☐ Categorise as: Choose category... ▼

[Create filter] ☐ Also apply filter to **35** matching conversations.

Learn more

FIGURE 8.3 **The next step in creating a filter**

any emails already in your account with these options.

To filter, click on **Create filter with this search**.

Figure 8.3 shows the next options available to you. You can archive it, mark it as read, star it, apply the label, and forward those particular emails to an email address and so on.

The most important options are **Apply the Label** and **Always/Never mark it as important**.

After clicking on **Create Filter**, you will get a confirmation screen to say it has been set up. The downside is that you will have to go through the process for each label as it doesn't allow you to choose more than one label at this stage.

If you are tidying up your emails and want to apply the label to all your previous emails then check the box next to **Create filter** which says **Also apply filter to X matching conversations.** If you are deleting all emails from a certain email address then all of the emails will be deleted not just future arrivals.

As can be seen above, you can do so much with filters, but what if you want to edit or delete a filter? Better yet, what if you have spent lots of time creating the best filters and you want to share them with a friend or vice-versa? Google has enabled them so that you can share with your friend (export filters) or have your friend share their filters with you (import filters). This section aims to show you how to do this.

Editing/changing a filter

If you think a filter is not appropriate any more you can

change the filter by clicking on the **Gear Wheel** > **Settings** > **Filters and Blocked Addresses** and clicking on **edit** next to the filter you want to tweak.

A word of warning, even if you change the filter and apply to all your emails, changes made by the previous filter will have to be dealt with on an email by email basis.

For example I had a filter in my test account which had everything from Ceri Clark go into a Friends/Ceri Clark label. All emails which had this label applied had these words in it. I then realized that the emails from Gmail which stated at the beginning 'Hi Ceri', were all labelled Friends/Ceri Clark. It included emails with just Ceri in. Adding quotation marks to the search had no bearing on the results so "Ceri Clark" still had emails with just Ceri sent to the label. Clearly inaccurate! I edited the label to have all emails sent from my email address to go to that label and all the right emails were now labelled correctly but of course the Gmail emails were still marked as from myself so I had to manually delete the labels from each email. The moral of this story is to think carefully about what labels to apply!

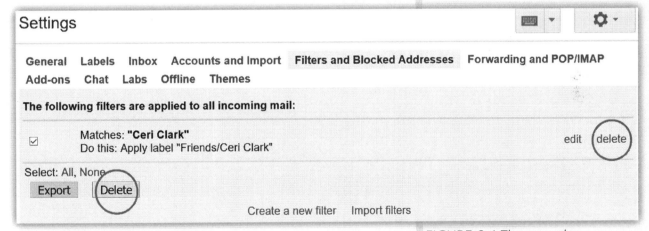

FIGURE 8.4 The two places to delete your filters in the **Filters and Blocked Addresses** settings page.

Deleting a filter

There are two places to delete your filters in the settings. Deleting a filter could not be simpler,

1. Go to the **Gear Wheel**
2. Click on **Settings**
3. Select **Filters and Blocked Addresses**

4. Click on **delete** on the far right of the filter you want to remove *or* check the box to the right of the filter and then click on the **Delete** button at the bottom of the Filters page in settings

Sharing filters with friends (exporting filters)

In order to export your filters, go to the filters section in settings (**Gear Wheel** > **Settings** > **Filters and Blocked**) and click on **Export** at the bottom of the page. Please see *figure 8.5* to see its location.

Once you have clicked on **Export** you will be asked to save the file on to your computer. The file will be downloaded with the extension of .xml. You can now email this filter to your friend.

FIGURE 8.5 Where to find Export.

Adding filters given to you (importing filters)

First go to **Gear Wheel** > **Settings** > **Filters and Blocked Addresses** and click on **Import filters (1)**. A new section will load at the bottom of the page which will look like this:

FIGURE 8.6 Importing filters

Click on **Browse (2)** and find the file named **MailFilters.xml** that you were given. Once you have clicked **Open** you will return to Google and you will need to click on **Open File (3)**.

The screen will reload with the filters that were in the file. You can stop at this point or you can choose which filters you want to import. Simply click on the little check-boxes next to the filters you want added to your account and click on **Create filters**. If you want the filters to apply to all the emails that are already in your account, click on the little box next to **Apply new filters to existing email**.

Google will automatically create the labels that are needed by the new filters.

Blocked addresses

Blocked addresses are a type of filter which is why they are grouped together in the **Filters and Blocked Addresses** section of Gmail settings. It is a quick way of setting up a filter to send all email from a certain email address to spam.

Blocking an address

1. From an opened email, click on the little arrow on the top right above your email as seen in *figure 8.7*
2. Look for **Block "x"** down the list and click on it
3. You will be warned that all emails from this person will go to Spam. Click **Block**

All emails from this person will now go directly to spam. If you are expecting an email you can check your spam to see if there are any emails there or unblock the address which is explained in the following section.

Unblocking an address

There may be a time when you want to unblock an address you have blocked in the past.

1. First go to **Gear Wheel**
2. Click on **Settings**

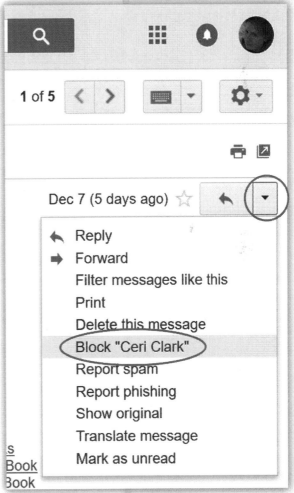

FIGURE 8.7 Blocking an address.

111

3. Choose **Filters and Blocked Addresses** and look down the page until you see **The following email addresses are blocked. Messages from these addresses will appear in Spam**

4. Either click on **unblock** to the right of the blocked address or check the box next to the blocked address on the left and then click on **Unblock selected addresses**

Create a new filter   Import filters

The following email addresses are blocked. Messages from these addresses will appear in Spam:

☑   **Ceri Clark** < arandomemailaddress >   unblock

Select: All, None

Unblock selected addresses

0 GB (0%) of 15 GB used   Terms - Privacy
Manage   Last account activity: 30 minutes ago
                                                                                              Details

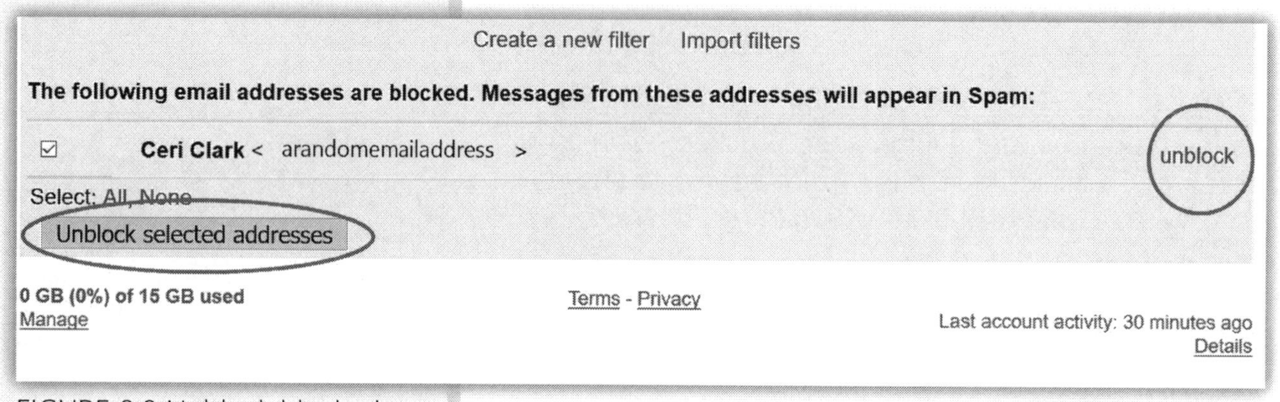

FIGURE 8.8 Unblock blocked addresses.

Chapter summary

Filters are a powerful tool for organizing your emails. In this chapter we discussed what filters are, how to set them up, how to edit them and how to delete them. Blocked addresses are another form of filter which simplifies creating a filter that sends all emails from an email address to spam. The last item in this chapter showed how to unblock any email addresses that has been blocked.

Chapter 09

Searching for, and in, Emails

What to expect in this chapter:

- Searching within your labels

- How to search for emails using an email address

- Searching your Sent emails

- Keyword searching

- Searching for emails with attachments

- Searching by size and date

- Sorting your emails by newest or oldest emails

Searching for your emails is a breeze with Gmail. In the basic sense all you need to do is type in your search term in the search box and then click on the magnifying glass for the Google search engine to search all your email for you.

FIGURE 9.1 Advanced search options can be found by clicking the arrow inside the search box.

Google does accept Boolean searching, for example using AND & OR, and quotes, but for a simpler way of powerful searching click on the little arrow inside the search box. If you hover your mouse over the arrow, you will get a little message stating **Show search options**. These are shown in *figure 9.2*.

The beauty of these options is that you can not only search from a particular email address but from emails which have certain words in them. Here are some tips for searching.

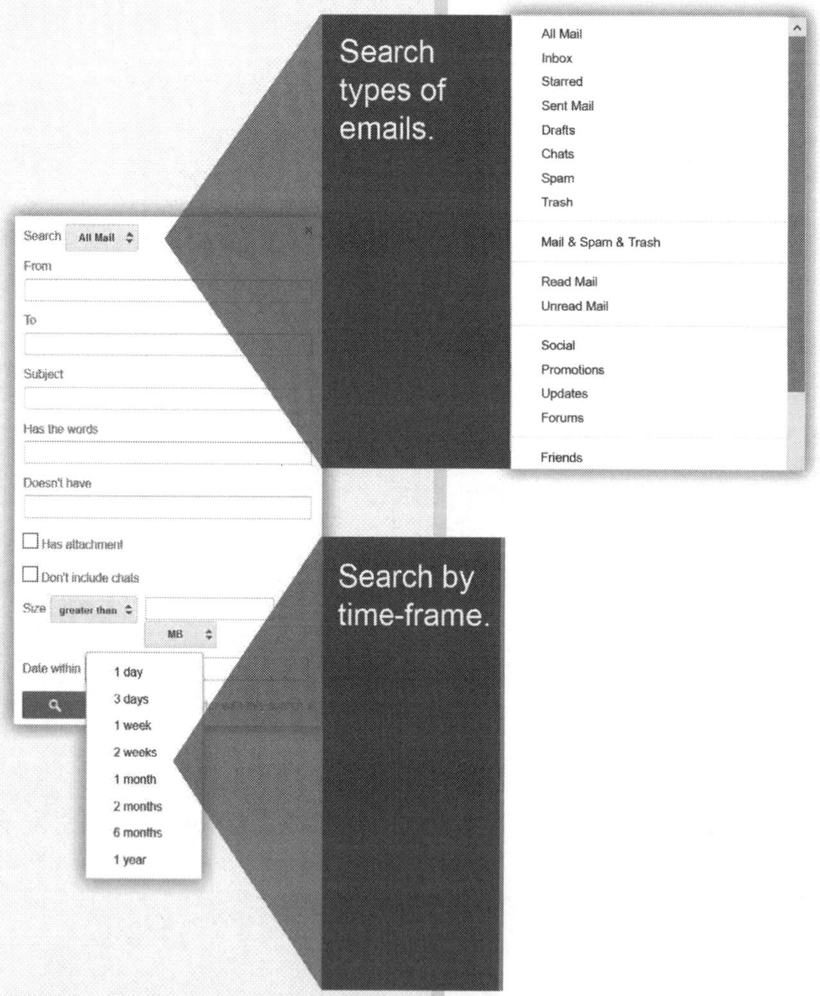

Searching in your labels

You can search only within a label by clicking the arrows next to **All Mail** in the search options and selecting the label you want to look in.

If you just type in the search box, Gmail will automatically search all your mail, but you can search in just the email you sent. Also, if you are organized and assigned all your emails labels then you can search within those. A possible scenario is that you may have a label for work related emails

FIGURE 9.2 **Advanced search options**

and another for personal. If this is the case you could just search in your personal emails if you needed to.

Searching for emails from a certain person

This can be done in two ways, you can just put the email address into the search bar, or the way I recommend is to go into the advanced search and type it into the **From** field (less room for error).

Searching emails you have sent to people

As above, you can type their email address straight into the search box or this time I recommend typing the email addresses into the **To** box in the advanced search.

Subject searching

When you type in the subject box, it will only search the subject of your emails. If you want to search for say, Washington but you don't want all those emails with Washington in the body of the email, this is the way to go.

This is great if you are getting a lot of emails with the same subject and you want to delete them. For example, you can search for Annoying Company Newsletter in the subject box and all their emails will be found. You can delete them at your leisure.

Searching for emails using keywords (Has the words...)

Whatever you are searching for, the **Has the words** field can be indispensable and with the help of the other boxes you can really narrow down your search.

An example would be if you were searching for the holiday company that you had a holiday with last year because

Did you know...

When you send emails try and make sure that the subject that you write is as descriptive of the content of your email as possible. Not only is this helpful for people receiving your email but when you want to find it again, Google will be able to find it easier if it has the right words in the subject.

09

115

you want to book with them again but you have forgotten what they are called.

You can remember you went to Orlando but the holiday company just eludes you. Type in the box Orlando and (if you kept it) Google will find your receipt email which would have the name of the company on it.

Removing emails from the search

The box labelled **Doesn't have** is one of the most useful options in Gmail search. You may be getting lots of emails in your search which are irrelevant but the search brings them up with the words you have put in. Finding words in the erroneous emails which tells you they aren't relevant and putting them in this box when you search again will remove them from your search.

Finding emails with an attachment

Ticking the box **Has attachment** will bring up results with only attachments. Gmail will also search within your attachments.

As an experiment I sent myself a document called Twinkle. docx. The email subject had Twinkle in the name and the content of the email simply stated Nursery Rhyme. The document itself had the full nursery rhyme, Twinkle, Twinkle, Little Star, typed out. I searched for star in my Gmail and although star was only mentioned in the actual document, Gmail put the email in the search results.

Searching through your Chats

Gmail will automatically search through your chats. If you tick the box labelled **Don't include chats**, Gmail will only search through your emails.

Searching by size

You can search for your emails by choosing greater than or less than a certain size of email. If you regularly send emails to a friend or colleague and they have sent you an attachment but you've lost the email, you can search for emails of a larger size to narrow your list.

Also, if you feel you are using too much space in your Gmail account, you can search for all emails over a certain size to find all emails with attachments. You can then delete emails which you think you no longer need to good effect. One email with an attachment can be worth hundreds of emails without them.

Another alternative is that if someone has sent you a document to your email that is large, you can save it to your Google Drive. You could convert it to a Google document format and delete the original. Information kept in Google's own file types such as Google Docs and Sheets do not count towards your space limits. If you are desperate for space this is a viable way of saving space without losing important documents.

Searching emails by date

The last option is to search within a time period. The options are within 1 day, 3 days, 1 week, 2 weeks, 1 month, 2 months, 6 months, and 1 year of a date you can select by clicking into the box next to this option. For example 1 year of 1 April 2017.

Alternatively, if you want a longer time period, you can type into the main search bar in the format:

after:2012/4/1 before:2014/4/2

Sorting emails by newest or oldest

Lastly in this chapter there is a little known trick for sorting

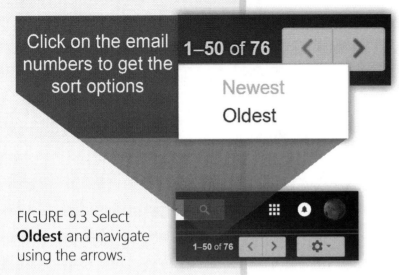

FIGURE 9.3 Select **Oldest** and navigate using the arrows.

your emails inside Gmail.

On the top right of your gmail account Gmail lets you know how many email are on the page you are viewing and how many emails you have in total. If you click on these numbers you can click **Oldest** to sort your emails so that you see the oldest first.

What this actually does is jump you to the page which has your oldest emails. It doesn't put your oldest emails on the first page but instead takes you to the last page. If you click on **Newest**, it will jump you right back to the beginning. The arrows next to the numbers allow you to navigate through your pages of emails.

You can choose how many emails you have in your page by going to the **Gear Wheel** > **Settings** > **General** > **Maximum page size:**

Select the number of conversations per page here from 10, 15, 20, 25, 50 and 100 per page.

Chapter summary

Gmail has powerful search functionality and you can choose to use more than one option to really narrow down your search. Search options include emails to and from a particular email address, the subject, keywords, attachments, size and date. There are also options for removing erroneous emails using *Doesn't have keywords* and then sorting your emails so you see the oldest first. Whether you use one or more of these functions in a search there is a combination that will help you to find what you need.

Chapter 10

Changing the Look and Feel

What to expect in this chapter:

- What is display density and what each option looks like

- How to change your background with themes

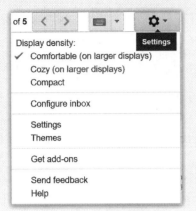

FIGURE 10.1 Location of Settings.

You've sent a couple of emails, told a few of your best mates about how great Gmail is but you're getting a bit bored with how it looks. This is the chapter to help you with this.

All of these changes can be made from **Settings**. This link can be found at the top right of the screen when you click on the gear wheel as illustrated in *figure 10.1*.

The Display Density

FIGURE 10.2 Density Display views

There are three options under **Display Density**. These are **Comfortable** (for larger displays), **Cozy** (again for larger displays) and **Compact**. Please see *figure 10.2* to see how each view compares side-by-side. They are designed to fit more or fewer emails depending on the size of the screen you are viewing your email on. The space between each email is larger with Comfortable, less in Cozy and in Compact view there is the least amount of space between emails.

Themes

To change the theme, choose **Themes** from under **Settings** under the gear wheel at the top right of the page. The themes can also be found as a tab at the top of the main settings page.

There are lots of themes to choose from and quite a few change automatically throughout the day, my particular favorite is the planets theme.

If you would like to use any of these themes, all you need to do is click on the square that represents them and they should be applied. There are a couple of themes that require you to let them know what country you are in but this is simply because the background picture changes according to the time of day (Mountains for example). It can be nice if you are stuck indoors with the curtains closed to know

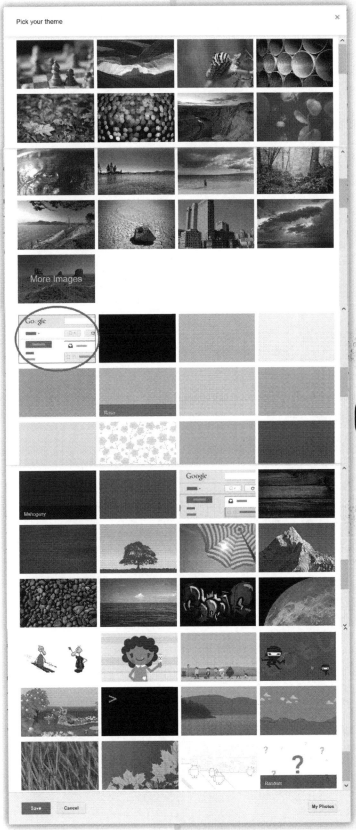

FIGURE 10.3 Themes available

121

that it is sunset because your Gmail background changes! If you want the original theme because you don't like the alternatives, choose the original, (the theme circled in *figure 10.3*), *Light theme*.

Try out the themes until you find one that you like. Sometimes a theme will make your navigation bar hard to see but you won't know until you try out a few. If there is one you particularly like but you are finding it hard to read the left menu, when you are choosing the theme, click on the square button with the circle inside it at the bottom of the pop up (the theme settings page). You can choose to add a vignette which can really make the text pop. Please see *figure 10.4* for how much of a difference this can make.

FIGURE 10.4 Before and after a vignette is added.

At the bottom of the themes pop up, you can choose to have your own photos as your Gmail background. Click on the button and browse your computer for your favorite photo.

Chapter summary

This chapter aims to give you a taste of how you can change the way Gmail looks to suit your personality. Change the density display to make it more comfortable to view and the theme to personalise it.

Chapter 11

Under the Hood - Gmail Settings

What to expect in this chapter:

- What is available in settings and how to use them

- Setting up your inbox view

- Accounts and Import, Forwarding and POP/IMAP

- Chat, Web clips and Offline

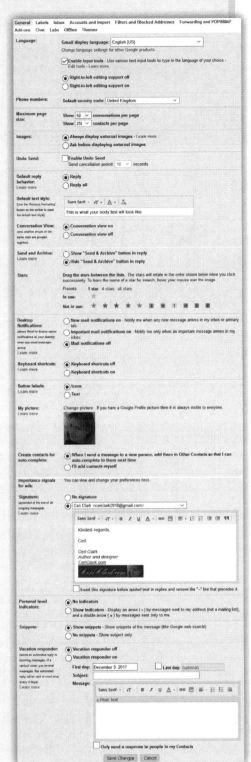

FIGURE 11.1 All the settings in the General tab.

This chapter covers all the settings under the general tab in the first instance but then goes into detail about inbox, importing and exporting to other email accounts, forwarding and POP/IMAP, chat, web clips and offline. Labs, labels and themes have their own chapters.

The General settings tab

The number of general settings can seem quite daunting when you first see them. This section aims to dispel the apprehension of seeing all those settings in one page. To get to these settings click on the gear wheel at the right of the screen and click on **Settings**.

Remember that if you make any changes you will need to scroll to the bottom of the page and click on **Save Changes** or the new setting will not apply.

Language

Choose the language appropriate to your region, for the US, US English is the default. UK users can choose the English (UK) option. If you communicate using Hindi, Arabic, or Chinese (or any other language that uses a different character set) then you will need to check the box next to **Enable input tools**. You should also check the box for right-to-left editing if your country's language requires this. Enable Input tools only works in the browser version of Gmail. Once it is enabled, you can get to it from the left of the gear wheel at the top right of your browser window.

Phone numbers

This option is to allow you to use Google Voice. While it is only available in limited places at the moment the option to choose so many countries suggests that Google are planning to roll out Google Voice to more places in the future.

Maximum page size

This option depends on how much you want to scroll, the more conversations and contacts you allow on each page the fewer pages you will have to click through but it also means you will have to scroll more.

You can limit your emails on a page to: 10, 15, 20, 25, 50, 100 emails.

You can limit your contacts to 50, 100, 250 contacts per page.

Images

This refers to displaying images within emails. While it is nice to see adverts in all their glory, in the past, if an email slipped through which had harmful code in it, malicious code could have damaged your computer. Now the setting is really for saving bandwidth and avoiding adverts. If this is what you want, click on **Ask before displaying external images**. If this drives you up the wall, you can always change to the other option again later.

Choose from:

- **Always display external images**
- **Ask before displaying external images**

Undo send

This is an invaluable and highly recommended setting. Have you ever sent an email and instantly regretted it or spotted a spelling mistake just as you clicked send? Check this box and it will give you a grace period where you can click on **undo** so it will never get sent. You can set the grace period to 5, 10, 20 or 30 seconds.

Default reply behavior

This option asks if you want to automatically reply to one person or all people in your email. I would strenuously

Always click on **Save Changes** at the bottom of the settings page to make them apply.

11

suggest that you choose **Reply**. You can always choose **Reply all** when you are typing the email but Gmail will automatically reply to just one sender email address if you click on just **Reply**.

I would not recommend **Reply all** as an automatic setting in any circumstances. It is easier to send an email again to people you have missed but very hard to make someone unsee an email!

It can seem very convenient to have a reply to all automatically done for you for every email you send. It means that no one would miss out on your emails if you are replying back, but if you are using your Gmail account for business purposes take the lessons learnt from big business that this may not be the best idea. The news has been full in the past of emails sent to the wrong people by accident and then forwarded on to strangers. The type of email that you shouldn't reply to all will usually find their way half-way across the world before you can say "*Oh dear what have I done*"! It is best to think before replying and think twice before replying to all.

Default text style

If you always want to send emails with the same formatting, for example Arial font or larger text size, then you can make this happen automatically from here. There are four main options: there is the font (e.g. Arial, Times New Roman etc.), the size of the text, (Small, Normal, Large and Huge), the color of your text and finally you can remove all formatting to bring the text in all your emails to the basic Gmail offering. Set the text to how you want it and all new emails you send including replies will use this automatically.

Conversation view

You can turn this off or on here. I would recommend you keep this on as it means you keep all your email about one 'subject' in one place. However, if you like all your emails separated so you can see everyone's replies on individual rows in your message list on your email homepage then you can turn it off here as well.

Send and archive

Enabling this function will add a button and save you a lot of time! With one click you can send a reply to an email while archiving at the same time. Without this, you can reply as normal but the email will stay in your inbox until you archive it manually. I highly recommend this button!

Stars

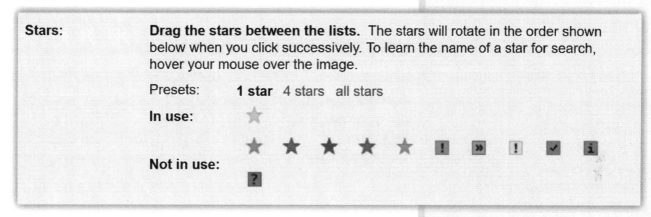

Stars are used to help organize your email. For example if you star an important email that you need to deal with by next week, then you can search for just starred emails. Use this section to choose what stars will be available. Drag the stars and symbols from the **Not in use** row to the **In use** row and click **Save changes** at the bottom of the page. To choose a different star, in your inbox click on the star symbol next to the email in the inbox. Keep clicking to get the different star and symbol options.

FIGURE 11.2 Drag the stars and symbols from the **Not in use** row to the **In use** row to use them.

11

Desktop notifications

If you are using the Google's Chrome, Mozilla's Firefox, Microsoft Edge or Apple's Safari browsers, then you can get notifications as pop ups to let you know when you have got new email. Your browser will prompt you to allow these notifications.

The options in Gmail are:

- **New mail notifications on - Notify me when any new message arrives in my inbox or primary tab.** This option will notify you of any new mail in your inbox but if you are using inbox categories then it will only let you know about new emails that are in your **Primary inbox**

- **Important mail notifications on - Notify me only when an important message arrives in my inbox.** You will only be notified of emails that have been marked important

- **Mail notifications off.** This will turn all desktop notifications off

Keyboard shortcuts

Turn these on or off depending on how much you want to use your mouse. I would recommend this is turned on so that you have the option to use shortcuts if you want to. A selection of shortcuts taken from the Google help pages are:

- To compose a message, type c, or Shift + c if you want it in a new window
- To return to the inbox type "u"
- To archive a message, type "e"
- To report spam, type "!"
- To bring up the label menu, type "l" (lowercase L)
- Add a Cc address to your email, type Ctrl + Shift + c (Mac: ⌘ + Shift + c)
- Add a Bcc address to your email, type Ctrl + Shift + b (Mac: ⌘ + Shift + b)
- To undo an action (it might not always work), type "z"

For all Google Gmail shortcuts, visit the Google help page at: http://support.google.com/mail/bin/answer. py?answer=6594

Button labels

If you find the icons too small or confusing, it is possible to change the navigation bar above your emails to have words instead of pictures. The next graphic illustrates how the two views compare. The text view will take up more

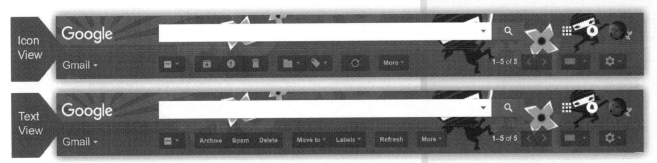

room in the Gmail specific navigation bar. You can make your browser bigger or smaller by clicking on Ctrl and using the scroll wheel on your mouse at the same time to compensate in Windows.

FIGURE 11.3 The difference between icon and text buttons.

My picture

In this section you can change the picture you selected during setup. Clicking on **Change picture** (above your photo) brings up a window where you can search your computer for your favorite picture of yourself. You can always use your cat's picture if you prefer!

For more in-depth guidance on adding/changing your picture, please refer to the **Adding your profile picture** in *Chapter 3*.

Create contacts for auto-complete

This is a great time saver. Instead of adding contacts manually, Gmail will add them automatically when you send an email to someone. Of course if you send a lot of emails to people you are sure that you never want to contact again then using the **I'll add contacts myself** option would be better.

If you want to find these contacts in Google Contacts, they are in the **Other contacts**, located under **More**. If you want them to appear in your main contacts list, just click on the **Add to contacts** button and it will move from **Other contacts** to your main list.

Important signals for ads

This setting is to show you what Google is using to target your adverts. When you click on the link you will be directed to a page which will show you what information Google is using and from where. You can choose what types of adverts are served to you and even what you don't want.

You can also opt-out of interest-based adverts. What this means is that you will still receive adverts but they won't be targeted and you can get anything. If you have to see adverts it is better that it is something you don't mind seeing. There are plugins to browsers which will block adverts, even Google ones, but that is not in the purview of this book.

Signature

Your signature is how you end your email, it saves you having to type the same information time and time again. You can just add text, your name, address, phone number etc., or you can even add images. The formatting options are above the typing window as it is in composing emails or in your standard word processor.

Detailed instructions for adding and formatting a signature can be found in *Chapter 5 (Sending and receiving emails)*.

Personal level indicators

I would recommend turning these on, but if you don't plan on joining any mailing lists, then this is not important. This could be a good indicator of spam. You would find out if the email was sent directly to you and not to a generic mailing list address before you opened it.

If you are using your account for business purposes then this is useful as an email sent only to you could be an indication of whether you have to action the email.

The options you can choose here are:

FIGURE 11.4 Signature example.

Did you know...

You can have different signatures for the different email addresses you have in Gmail.

If you set up the **Send mail as** option in **Accounts and Import** then you can choose an option in the dropdown box (under No signature) to set up a different signature for each email address you can send from.

- **No indicators**
- **Show indicators** - Displays an arrow (›) by messages sent to my address (not a mailing list), and a double arrow (») will be by messages sent only to me.

Snippets

This option is a matter of personal preference. If you check your email in a public place then you may prefer to have this switched off. What it does is put the first line of your email viewable from the inbox. It can be a time saver as it tells you what is new in a conversation at first glance but it can also let other people looking over your shoulder know a little of what has been sent to you. The choice is yours.

Vacation responder/Out of office auto-reply

This section is very useful in a business context. It allows you to tell your contacts that you are not available when you are on holiday or if you are indisposed. If you want to use this for your holidays, remember to click on **Only send a response to people in my Contacts**. You don't want potential burglars knowing you are on holiday or spammers/hackers knowing you might not be checking your email!

You can schedule the message so it will be sent while you are away and automatically turn off when you are back.

Another possible (business) use is as an auto responder if you were to not include an end date. You can write a message such as *"Thank you for your email. Your message is important to us and we will get back to you as soon as possible."*

Again you can restrict this message to people in your contacts if you put phone numbers and other contact details you may not want generally known.

11

The Labels tab

I have gone into more depth in *Chapter 7: Email organization with labels*, but if you have jumped to this section, basically think of them as folders but where one email can be in several folders/places at the same time.

This is the place where you can organize your emails by specifying what labels i.e. 'folders' you want to see in the left column. I would suggest you need the **Sent Mail**, **Drafts**, **All Mail** and **Trash/Bin** and add anything else when and as you need it.

The Inbox tab

The inbox settings are Google's way of organizing your emails for you. If don't want to use filters, using Google's Inbox feature can de-clutter your main inbox window without any effort other than choosing which of their categories you want to use.

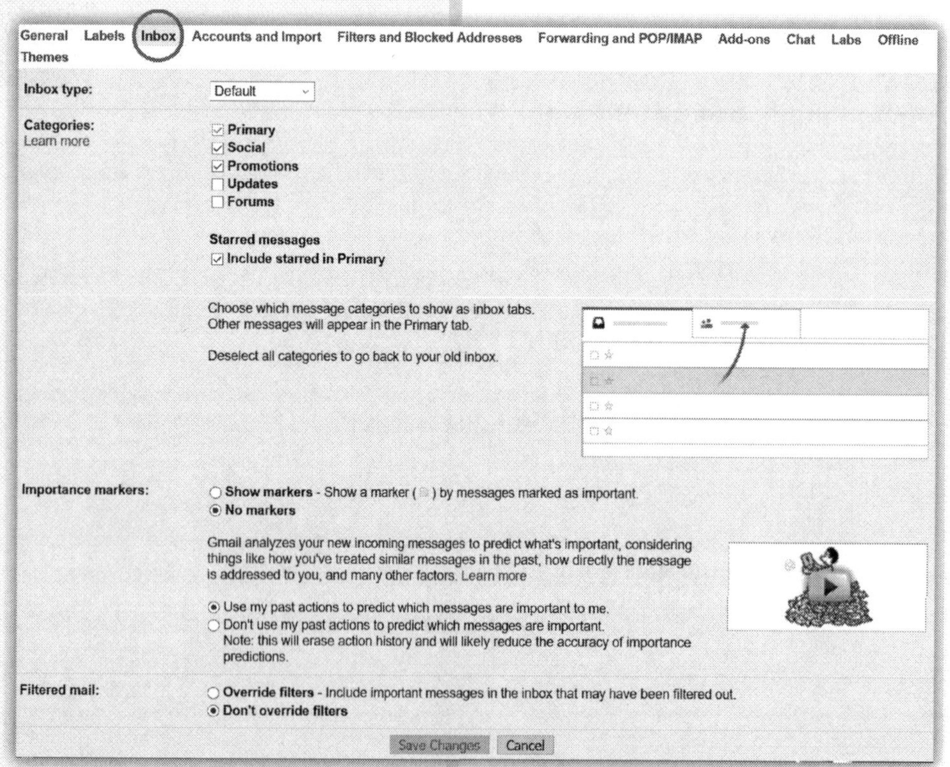

The first options that you will see are the inbox types. You can customize how your inbox is organized using these. The different inbox types will change what you see in this settings page. The inbox types are:

- Default
- Important first
- Unread first
- Starred first
- Priority inbox

Each option has their own particular look and functionality. Try

FIGURE 11.5 Inbox tab overview.

them all out to see which suits you best. I will talk in more details about each type next.

Default

If you choose default next to inbox type, then you can choose which categories you want to activate (if any). If you do choose default and categories I would strongly suggest that you also check the box next to **include starred in Primary**, simply for the reason if you have gone out of the way to star it or make a filter to do it then you clearly want to see it as a priority. You wouldn't want your starred email to be buried in social for example.

When you choose **Default** you can choose what gmail category inboxes you want to implement. Here is a break down.

Gmail's category inboxes (tabs)

Google has a set of category inboxes which can be used to automatically categorise your emails as they come in. They will appear above your message list on the homepage and all you need to do is click on the tab to see the emails.

You can activate or remove Gmail category inboxes (which appear as tabs above your message list) from two places:

> **Location 1. Gear Wheel > Configure inbox**

> **Location 2. Gear Wheel > Settings > Inbox (as long as Default is selected in the first option)**

To configure your inboxes, you need to use the inbox types detailed in the section in the **Inbox tab** located in the main Gmail settings.

The primary tab

Your primary tab, is the first tab you will see when you open your inbox. It should have all the emails that Google thinks are important to you. If Google cannot classify emails, then they will also go into here.

Did you know...

If you just want one inbox without any tabs, simply choose default and then uncheck all the categories.

11

133

The social tab

Google will put any emails from social networks in this tab to stop them cluttering up your primary inbox. These can be from Facebook and Twitter to Goodreads.

The promotions tab

The promotions tab is for all those emails offering you deals on your favorite stores that you signed up for in the past. If you don't want these but you remember signing up in the first place then you can usually unsubscribe by going to the bottom of the open email to locate and click on the word **unsubscribe**. If you didn't sign up for the emails then feel free to mark them as spam. There are instructions for how to do this in *chapter 4 Security*.

The updates and forums tab

The emails categorized as updates are usually confirmations, receipts, bills, and statements. Emails put into the forums category are usually from mailing lists or forums.

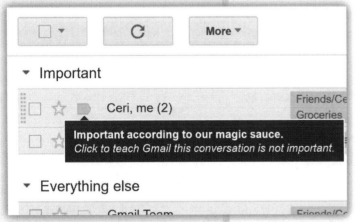

FIGURE 11.6 Click on the arrow to show it is not important.

Important first

The **Important first** inbox type puts important emails at the top and everything else below. This has the benefit of only having the one inbox. However you will have to trust what Google considers important mail. Creating filters for emails you know are coming could affect this.

If you only have a few emails, then this could be the answer. If you have been using your Gmail account for a while and have consistently organized your email with filters and generally used your account, Google will be able to make more accurate guesses for what is important to you.

If you hover your mouse over the yellow arrow next to the check box in your email discussion, Google will explain why it thinks the emails are important. You can click on the arrow to let Gmail know it isn't important.

The different options in the Inbox unread count didn't change the inboxes in the tests I undertook so I would leave these options as they are when you find them.

Unread first

The **Unread first** inbox type does what it says. Any email that you have not read yet will appear at the top of your inbox. Again, you will only have the one inbox to look through. This is a good way to use Gmail if you use your email with a task based approach (you assess an email and deal with it immediately or later). With this option you will see new emails first and can deal with these straight away. After this you can tuck in to the emails that you have read but that don't need immediate action.

The different options in the Inbox unread count didn't change the inboxes in the tests I undertook so I would leave these options as they are when you find them.

Starred first

All emails that you star or have starred by Gmail using filters will appear at the top of the list and everything else separated underneath. This option also means that you only have the one inbox to look through.

If you have a lot of starred emails, it could get a little annoying to scroll through lots of email before you get to new emails. However if you star emails you are working on or only have a few, then this could be a good option for organizing your email.

It is possible to prioritize your starred email by clicking on the star beside the email you want to mark important. By clicking on the star you will scroll through the options you set in the general settings. As you can see in *figure 11.7*, Gmail will group the stars of the same type together. If any email are marked important then they will still rise to the

FIGURE 11.7 Starred emails are grouped together unless they are marked as important.

11

135

top of the list.

The order that you have the stars in the settings will set the importance in the starred list. The first stars are the least important while the last star you drag and drop will become the most important.

Priority inbox

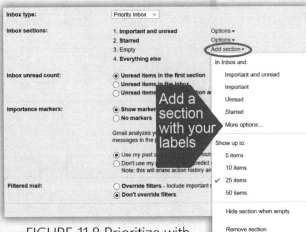

FIGURE 11.8 Prioritize with your own labels.

This leaves the Priority inbox. In this view items that Google thinks are most important will appear at the top. Click on **Priority inbox** next to the inbox type to activate it and then **Save Changes**.

Even though Google will try to prioritize your email, you can also dictate inbox sections by clicking on **Options** next to the appropriate section (see *figure 11.8* for more details).

If you click on **Options** or **Add section**, you will have the options above. You can choose the Gmail standard inbox settings or you can add your own section based on labels you have created. You can also choose how many emails will be displayed and whether you want to hide or remove a section.

When you click **Save Changes**, your inbox will instantly show the changes you made.

Your inbox can be customized further, once you have chosen the priority inbox. You can choose how it is laid out with the following sections:

- Important and unread
- Starred
- Empty
- Everything else

By clicking on **Options** to the right of these sections you can change how many emails appear in each section. The third section can be the most powerful and interesting way of how you can personalize Gmail. Click **Add Section** and you can choose a label as a section under **More options**. This means that you can have all your emails about a

136

certain subject right there in full view in your inbox. If you have set up filters so that your inbox is bypassed, you will see the newest five emails on the subject of your choice.

You can bypass filters by using the **Filtered mail** section of the inbox settings. This will include emails that Google feels is important to you even if you have filtered them out.

Accounts and import

This section is for changing your password, importing your old email from another provider, changing how your name appears when someone gets your email, granting access to your account and adding storage.

FIGURE 11.9 Accounts and Import Overview

137

Change account settings

You should always have different passwords for different websites. However, Google allows you to have one password for all of its services. For the purposes of your password, Gmail, Google Drive, Google Docs, Google Sheets etc. *are all one website*. You will need to change this password from time to time. Perhaps it has been used on a different website such as a store and has been compromised, or the password just needs changing. Clicking on **Change password** allows you to do this.

If you forget your password you will need to have made sure that your recovery settings are updated. The second option (**Change password recovery options**) in this section will take you to a page where you can tell Google about a phone number or an alternative email address in the rare circumstance that you have forgotten your password. This is very important because if something happens to your account you will not be able to get in unless you set up the recovery options.

The **Other Google Account settings** points to a menu page where you can access your Google account settings which will affect all Google services including Google Drive, Docs, Sheets, Gmail etc. It is worth having a look around these pages even though they are not strictly Gmail related.

Import mail and contacts

Please see *Importing mail and contacts in Chapter 3 Getting Started* for detailed instructions for how to import your emails and contacts from other email addresses you have previously owned.

You can stop the importing (if you took the option to import new messages daily for 30 days) by clicking on **stop** to the right of the email address or import from another address you may have by following the instructions again.

Send Mail As

You may have several email addresses which you may want to keep but only wish to send email from your Gmail account. This can be done in the **Accounts and Import** section under **Send mail as**. This will mean that you can choose to send from email addresses you already have access to, which will make the recipient think you sent it from somewhere else. It also means that all your sent email will be in the one place for ease of searching.

Send Mail As may not work for all your other accounts. For example, for this book I tested a Gmail and a Yahoo account for this feature. While the other Gmail account worked perfectly the first time, the Yahoo account refused to work until I allowed **apps that use less secure sign-in** to access it. If you do try out these instructions and they do not work, you can use Gmailify which in effect does the same thing. When it is set up and you send an email from Gmail (selecting your yahoo account as the from address), when the recipient gets the email it will look like it was sent from your Yahoo account. This means that Gmailify is an alternative if **Send Mail As** does not work for a particular email. Please see **Check mail from other accounts (using POP3 & Gmailify)** in the next section for instructions on how to get to and use *Gmailify*.

As you would expect the email address you just created is already there. To add another one, click on **Add another email address** you own. A pop up will appear giving you a wizard to follow:

1. Enter your name and email address that you already own or have permission to access

2. Decide what name you want to be displayed in your recipient's email software against your emails. Tick the box (**Treat as an alias**), if you are emailing on someone else's behalf or one of your other email addresses and you want replies to go to the other inbox and not yours)

3. Type in your password and click on **Next Step**

4. Check the information you type in your password before clicking on **Add account**

5. Verify your email address. Enter the verification

Did you know...

Other email providers may stop you from importing information as a security feature. Yahoo is one of these. If you want to import emails and contacts from Yahoo *and it is not working* then you will have to enable a feature to allow this to work. Here's how to do this:

- Login in to Yahoo mail

- Click on your name at the top right of the screen

- Click on **Account info**

- Click on **Account security**

- Enable **Allow apps that use less secure sign-in**

The steps listed should now work.

11

If you or someone else is sending as an alias please be aware that the sent email will not be duplicated across accounts. This means that the email will not be in both sent items but will only appear in the email account you are emailing from, not the one you are pretending to email from.

code that Google has sent to your other email address. Google does not want unauthorized people sending from other accounts. It also ensures that if someone tried to do this for your account without you knowing you are notified that someone is trying to access it. You or the person you are allowing access to your account will receive an email checking to see if they are okay with this. They or you need to click the confirmation link in the email address. If there is a problem with the link, there is a verification code as well. The easiest way by far is to click the link though

6. Once you have verified the access, log back in to your Gmail account. If you go back to your **Accounts and Import** section in the settings you will see **make default**, **edit info** and **delete**. Only click on **Make default** if you want this to be your primary address, the one that you want to receive and send emails with. Otherwise you will get the option of which email you want to use each time you compose an email

7. Make sure under the **When replying to a message** that you choose the **Reply from the same address to which the message was sent**. Otherwise, life can get very confusing for you and your recipient. They won't know where they should be emailing and you may give out an email address you wouldn't want a stranger, for example, to know about

You are now set up. When you next compose a message in the **From** field where your email address appears, you can now select the new address if you so wish simply by selecting the little arrow to the right of the email address.

Check mail from other accounts (using Gmailify & POP3)

Gmailify and POP3 are other ways of sending and receiving emails from another account. Even more ways are to a) import your emails and contacts and either use your new email address as is, and b) use the **Send mail as** featured through Gmail.

Using POP3 to import email means that you can import

the email from other email addresses you have just created or from another address to this one on a regular basis but all folders won't be the same on *every* device you use. If you send from a different device then the emails from that device won't be replicated in your webmail account for example. You won't have copies everywhere.

Gmailify means you can send email from your Gmail account but it will look like it was from your other account. The emails will be the same in your other account, e.g. be in the **Sent Mail** and your will get the great spam protection that Gmail offers.

IMAP is a similar solution to Gmailify which means there is a two way communication between the locations. Instead of just having your email 'pushed' to your new address, with IMAP your sent and received emails will be synchronized. This means if you are using IMAP and you are using Outlook to send emails, the emails you send will be identical on the web version of Gmail and also on your Android/Apple phones (if you use them).

Because of the inbuilt Gmail features available to Gmailify, it is the best option if you want to look like you are using your other address.

On the other hand, you may as well just use Gmail on the web for convenience if you don't want to use Gmailify, IMAP, POP3 or Send Mail as.

If you do decide you want to use POP3, then please see the following tutorial. You can add up to five accounts.

Gmailify instructions

Using Gmailify has the same first few steps as the POP3 option.

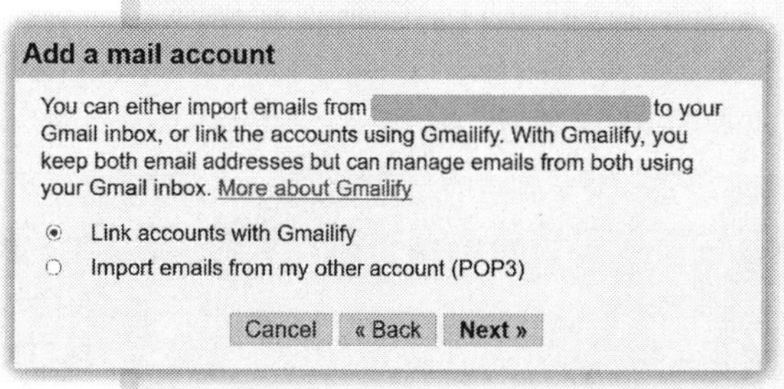

1. Type in the email address that you want to import from and click on **Next** (*figure 11.10*)
2. Click on **Link accounts with Gmailify** (*figure 11.11*).
3. Click on the account you want to link

141

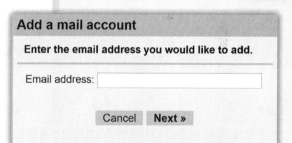

FIGURE 11.10 Step 1 is to type in your email address.

FIGURE 11.11 Link your accounts or implement POP3.

4. Sign in to your other email account
5. Click on **Agree**. You will see the following message:

You've been Gmailified!

You can now manage your yourotheremailaddress emails from Gmail. Better spam protection and email categories will help keep your inbox clean.

Your account should then be linked and you will be able to check this in the Gmail settings. To use your linked email account when you next compose a new message, click on the **From** box and choose the email address from the selection.

You can unlink at any time by going to **Settings** in Gmail.

POP3 instructions

Please note if you are importing from another Gmail account you will need to make sure that POP email is enabled from **Gear Wheel** > **Settings** > **Forwarding and POP/IMAP**. This is an important security feature as this setting could be used by hackers. Google has bypassed this by making sure you are the one to enable the feature.

1. Type in the email address that you want to import from and click on **Next**
2. Click on **Import emails form my other account (POP3)**
3. Type in your username and password and select what you want Gmail to do to your emails and click on **Add Account**

Using Gmail for work?

Google does ask if you are using Gmail for work and refer you to their apps accounts. They do not guarantee anything with a free account. After all it is free and they are running a business. If you want more 'protection' then a paid apps system may be the way to go. Gmail can be sufficient for sole traders but you would need to read the terms and conditions of use to make a fully informed decision of what service you want to use.

Grant access to your account (Delegation)

Another interesting and useful feature is **Grant Access to your Account**. This should only be done where there is the utmost trust involved but if you have a family member who doesn't really use email but they still need an account then this is a great way to help them. Another possible use is if you are a couple and want to use one account for accessing services. Instead of setting up forwarding for the emails sent by your electricity supplier why not have a joint account to which you both have access? You can of course remove access by a click of a button if you need to regain control.

Add additional storage

When you have used your account for some time, you may feel you need more space. Click on **Purchase additional storage** for the latest prices and limits on offer by Google.

Filters and blocked addresses

Please see **Chapter 8 Filters and Blocked Addresses** for more information on this. If you just need to find them, go to the gear wheel on the top right of the screen >**Settings** > **Filters and Blocked Addresses**.

Forwarding and POP/IMAP

It is possible to forward all your email to another email address. For example if you would like your email to be forwarded to your work email address, then this is one possible way.

To find the options go to the gear wheel on the top right of the screen > **Settings** > **Forwarding and POP/IMAP** as illustrated in the next image.

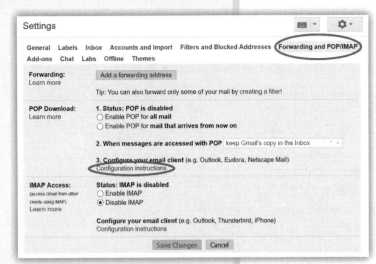

FIGURE 11.12 Forwarding and POP/IMAP overview

Forwarding

To add a forwarding address:

1.   Click on the gray box with the words **Add a forwarding address**. A pop up will appear asking you to add an address, type it in

2.   Click **Next**

3.   Click on **Proceed** and then **OK** and then go to the email account you specified

4.   Click on the link in the email sent to you from Gmail. A confirmation in a browser window will let you know you have been successful. If the link doesn't work, you will be able to use the code in the same email to confirm that the other email address is happy to receive the emails

POP download

POP mail is used for downloading into a desktop email application such as Outlook, Thunderbird, Postbox or MacMail. If this is a new email account, enabling POP for all mail if you want to use Outlook or another desktop client can be a good option. I would also recommend Archiving Gmail's copy in the drop down box. This means that when you visit the web version of Gmail you won't be overwhelmed with new email. You will know that it has been downloaded by the fact it is no longer in the inbox.

If you want to configure the settings on your particular email software, click on **Configure instructions** as seen in *figure 11.12*.

IMAP access

This is recommended over POP as instead of simply downloading your emails you can interact and sync it with both your email desktop application such as Outlook etc., apps on your mobile devices and the web version of Gmail. This means that if you move an email in Outlook

Did you know...

You can forward specific emails by using filters instead of forwarding all your emails. For example you might find this useful if you want to forward copies of all emails from a utilities company to your partner/spouse.

144

to a folder it will appear labelled in Gmail as well as other ways of accessing your email and vice-versa.

Make sure IMAP is enabled by clicking **Enable IMAP** and then remember to save any changes you've made.

The key settings to remember for setting up your IMAP access on your device is imap.gmail.com using port 993 (with SSL) for the incoming server and the outgoing server should be smtp.gmail.com on port 587 (with SSL).

If you are using an apps account, then you will need the same settings. The device you are using may try to use the domain from your email address but ignore this and put the Gmail information in. For example don't let it put in imap.yourdomain.com, it should be imap.gmail.com.

Add-ons

Add-ons are plugins that extend the functionality of Gmail. These are not made by Gmail and by adding these, you are giving third parties access to your account. They could, however streamline your working life from within Gmail, so it may be worth your while taking a look at some of these. Here is a brief description of the add-ons available at the time of writing. The list of add-ons in Gmail will change over time, more will be added and others taken away. Some apps are only available in certain countries.

To uninstall any of the add-ons, go to the **Gear Wheel** > **Settings** > **Add-Ons** > **Manage** (the add-on) > **Options** > **Remove**.

Asana for Gmail Converts emails into tasks that can be worked on by a team to facilitate projects.

BuiltWith The BuiltWith add-on tracks technologies linked to the domains on emails you receive. This will give you information about the domain sending you emails.

Dialpad This is a phone service that works from inside Gmail using Google Voice.

Groove Gmail Add-on This application integrates your Groove and Salesforce accounts with Gmail, connecting your CRM, inbox and calendar.

Hire This add-on is to help you in the recruitment process for your organisation. It integrates with G-Suite tools such as Google Search, Gmail, Calendar, Docs, Sheets and Hangouts to streamline the hiring process.

MeisterTask for Gmail Use your MeisterTask account to turn emails into tasks and insert them into your project. The subject line and text content of the email will automatically be added to your task.

Pod for Gmail A scheduling application that allows you to see past and upcoming events for the people emailing you.

ProsperWorks CRM Add-on for Gmail Prosperworks (CRM) links with Gmail so that you can view contact and activity details about individuals from within your emails.

RingCentral for Gmail With your RingCentral account, you can see the online/offline status of your RingCentral contacts within your email threads in Gmail. From your emails, it allows you to take a look at their recent call history, make calls, and view and send SMS messages.

Smartsheet for Gmail Add-On Adds emails to spreadsheets. Add rows, comments and organize your attachments.

Sortd Gmail Add-on A light-weight CRM. This is a collaboration and organizational tool.

Streak CRM Add-on for Gmail Streak is designed for Sales, Recruiting, and Customer Support.

Trello for Gmail Converts your emails into tasks.

Wrike for Gmail Create and manage your tasks from your emails with Wrike.

Chat

If you enable this option then I would recommend you choose **Save chat history** so you have a record of what is said. You can always turn this off but if you need a 'paper trail' then this would let you know what was said and when.

146

Labs

I would ignore this setting until you are completely familiar with the Gmail system. For more information on these, please see *Chapter 18 Gmail Labs*.

Offline

Only enable this if you have an unsteady internet connection or none for periods of time. Gmail is designed to be used online and works best this way.

Themes

There is more information on themes in *Chapter 10 Changing the Look and Feel*. However if you have jumped to this section you can change your theme by clicking on the picture you like in:

Gear wheel > **Settings** > **Themes**

Chapter summary

This is one of the largest chapters in this book as the settings have a wide ranging effect on Gmail and Google's other services. Many of the settings even have their own chapters in this book. Where information is discussed in more depth, the chapters are shown.

All the tabs within settings are explained within this chapter which include:

- General
- Labels
- Inbox
- Accounts and Import
- Filters and Blocked Addresses

- Forwarding and POP3/IMAP
- Add-ons
- Chat
- Labs
- Going Offline and
- Themes

Chapter 12

Email Management

What to expect in this chapter:

- Strategies for time management

- Blending Gmail tools to best organize your emails

Spending time setting up Gmail is only the beginning of keeping your email under control. If you have set up filters, labels and your settings correctly then you will only need to spend a few minutes each day going through what is important with a few more minutes to deal with non-urgent matters.

Time management

To really get to grips with your emails, I would suggest spending 10 minutes of your time each morning to deal with your emails and an hour on a Monday or Friday morning to attend to new emails and keep them organized.

To make good use of your time, I recommend turning off email notifications. Before you say, "but I need to know when they arrive," do you? If you can schedule a time or times each day to check your mail, then you can give your emails the attention they deserve. You will be able to check when you are ready and not be at the mercy of your email.

Prioritize, prioritize, prioritize

I can't stress enough how important prioritization is for an organized inbox. Google gives you several tools for this, which includes filters but starring emails will prioritize emails within inboxes, whether created by Google or yourself.

Starring emails

Star emails to be actioned. You can have different stars for how urgently the emails need to be dealt with. For example, an exclamation mark (this is still classed as a star), would be emails that need to be actioned within the next couple of days, a red star within the week, a blue star within the month and a yellow star to be dealt with by the end of 6 months. Anything that has to be sorted out immediately should already have been sorted out in your primary inbox.

If you can, set up filters that will automatically star email and sort them into the appropriate inbox. When you have dealt with your really urgent emails you will know that the less urgent emails will be there waiting and you will have a starting point for prioritizing further.

Replying to messages

Knowing which emails you need to reply to can save you time. If you have been sent an email but it wasn't directed at you i.e. you were in the cc: box, the email is probably just for information. The sender will probably be very happy not to receive 200 messages from every recipient saying that they have received it.

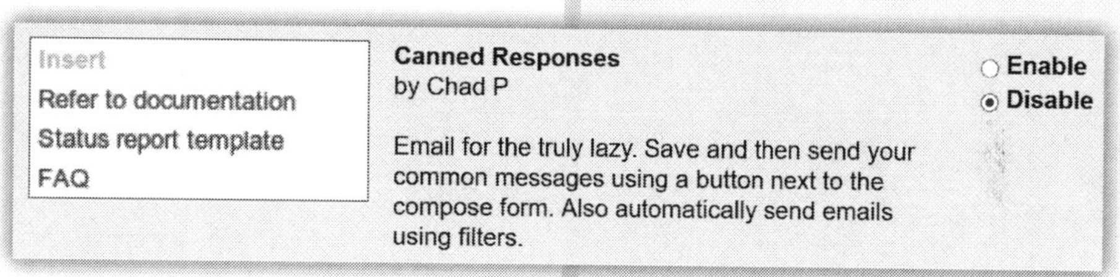

You don't have to reply to every message that needs to be actioned straight away but you can use **Canned messages** to say thank

you for your email (and that you will be dealing with it soon) using a filter to automatically send replies.

FIGURE 12.1 Enable **Canned Responses** from **Labs** in **Settings**.

If you want to enable the canned response lab, go to the cog or gear wheel on the top right of your Gmail screen, click on **Settings** then **Labs**. Find **Canned Responses** and select **Enable** before clicking on **Save Changes** at the bottom of the page.

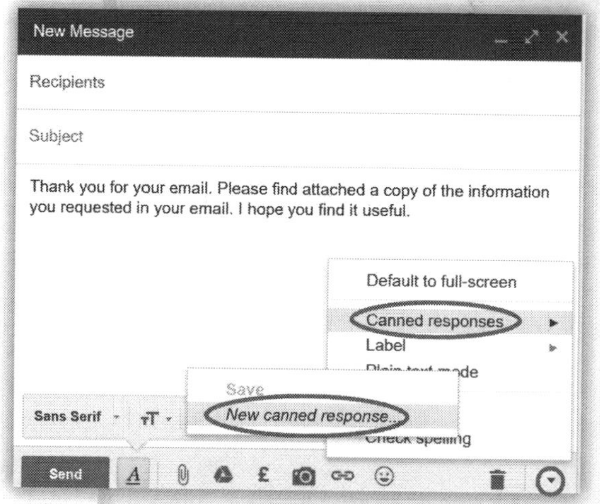

Now that Canned Responses is available on your Gmail account, start a new email and type in what you want in your canned reply into the email. This will become your template. You can use the usual formatting options, for example, bold, italics as well as including pictures and links. Remove any signature that you have set up in this email otherwise when you insert a new canned response you will get two signatures in the email.

FIGURE 12.2 Create a canned response from a new message.

On the bottom right of the email next to the picture of the trash can/bin, you will see a little arrow pointing down. Select this and click on **New canned response...**

151

A new window will load, prompting you to name your canned response. Choose a name that resonates with you. You might make a lot of these and you will want to be able to find it later.

If you made the canned message in response to a message, go ahead and click on **Send**. If you created the message from scratch to make a canned response to be used for later, delete the message you created. It will now be in your canned responses.

Replying with a Canned Response

Click on **Reply** or start a new message. Go to the bottom right of your message and click on the little arrow next to the trash can/bin. Select **Canned Responses** and then choose a response from the list that you want to reply with, *figure12.3* illustrates how to do this.

Editing/Overwriting a Canned Response

Unfortunately you cannot actually edit a canned response but you can overwrite it. Simply follow the steps to create a canned response as detailed above and then click on the name of the canned response (under the light gray **Save** in the list).

Deleting Canned Responses

Deleting a canned response is similar to overwriting one. Go to the little arrow on the bottom right of a new email. Click on **Canned responses** and then choose the canned response you want to delete under the light gray **Delete** as can be seen in *figure 12.3*.

Using filters to automatically send Canned Responses

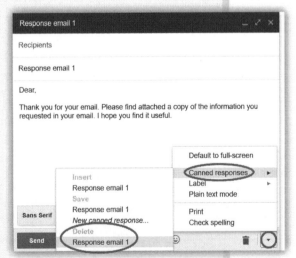

FIGURE 12.3 Where to delete a canned response.

If you have several canned responses, you can filter your emails so that when you get emails that meet certain

152

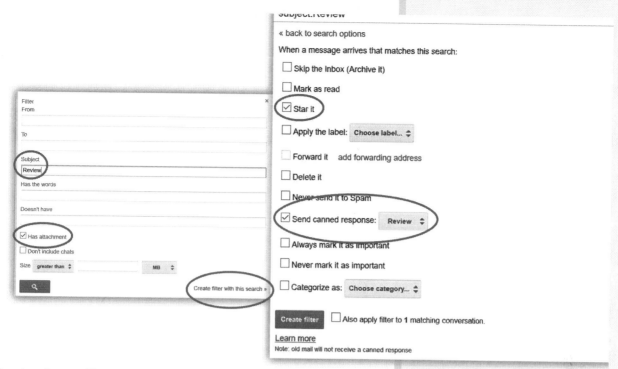

criteria, they will get a canned response automatically.

In the following example I will walk you through how I would send canned responses to emails that I receive for review copies.

1. Create your canned response (please see my instructions on how to do this earlier in the chapter)
2. Go to the cog/gear wheel (top right of Gmail screen)
3. Choose **Settings**
4. Click on **Filters**
5. Scroll down and click on **Create a new filter** (bottom of screen)

For this example I typed in **Review** in the subject and checked the box labelled **Has attachment**. You can just as easily put in email addresses.

6. Click on **Create filter with this search**
7. On the next screen check the box next to **Send canned response** and choose the one you want to send for your search

In the above example I checked next to **Star it**. You can also **Always mark it as important**. Another option is to

FIGURE 12.4 Creating a filter with a canned response.

12

skip the inbox if the email needs acknowledgement but you don't need to do anything.

8. Click on **Create filter**

Now any email that has review in the subject and also has an attachment will automatically get the canned response I selected.

Using the inbox tabs

The goal is to have only the important unread emails that you need to deal with in your inbox. Anything else should be in folders (labels) that you deal with when you have time.

Creating folders for your messages which do not have to be dealt with as soon as you open Gmail will mean that you will work on what matters first and then the rest in order of priority. While you can have several folders within folders for example, Newsletters, then Business Week Daily and possibly Reuters Money which could be Newsletters/BusinessWeekDaily and Newsletters/ReutersMoney, the aim is to quickly check these folders daily so you don't want to make work for yourself. I recommend having no more than three extra folders. Simplicity is the key. If you have too many folders and it gets too complicated, you just won't do it anymore. There are always far too many interesting things to do than dealing with your Gmail. Before I streamlined my email, my house received a regular lovely spring clean as a delaying tactic. My house is no longer as tidy but my email is now ultra organized!

The three labels/folders I would suggest are:

1. Pending
2. For Information
3. Newsletters

The **Pending** folder will contain all the email that you need to deal with that are not important enough to be in the Primary inbox, starred by importance.

The **newsletters** folder/label would have all your newsletters from different sources. Chances are you will

<u>Did you know...</u>

If there are emails in the wrong tabs, then all you need to do is grab the email using your mouse and drag it to the appropriate tab before dropping it in it. You will be asked if you want all future emails from that address put into the new tab. I would recommend you do so unless the email you are dropping into it is a one-off.

not have time to read all the newsletters anyway as there are always more coming in than there is time to read. Just pick the most recent or that look the most interesting and delete the rest. Be honest with yourself, are you really going to read all those newsletters?

The **For Information** folder is for all email that you have been CC'd in. If you have been cc'd then the email was not sent to you directly. This means you can class it as not urgent because presumably whoever it was directed to is dealing with it. This means they can wait until you have time to look at them.

Your aim is that the above three folders should only have active emails in. If you only want to keep it in case you need it, file it somewhere. These folders are there to organize your mail not as storage. Set aside up to an hour on a Monday or Friday morning to sort emails out each week. If you follow all the advice in this book it could be reduced to as little as ten minutes. It will make you feel a lot better to finish the week or begin the week all organized!

Other Folders

Labelling is essential to keeping your emails organized in Gmail. Once emails have been dealt with and archived, you may want to get hold of them again. It will be a lot more efficient to find an email if you can search within a label as your Gmail account fills up.

Another reason to have other folders apart from having the inboxes as described earlier in this chapter is for family emails that you don't want distracting you during your working day.

Using filters with labels

I go into great depth on how to use filters in *Chapter 8 Filters and Blocked Addresses* but if you only use filters with labels then you will still go a long way to organizing your mail. If you want to assign the label **Jobs** to all emails from your contact Jenny@WorkCorp.com, then go to:

the **cog/gear wheel** at the top right of the screen > **Settings** > **Filters and Blocked Addresses** > **Create a new filter**.

Type @WorkCorp.com (in case your contact from the company changes) into the **From** box and then click on **Create filter with this search**.

On the next screen check the box next to **Apply the label** and if you haven't already created the label, choose

FIGURE 12.5 Creating a filter to add labels.

Did you know...

You can use **Filter messages like these** to delete a lot of emails from the same person at once. Check on an email in your inbox, Select **More** then **Filter messages like these** and then click on **Search** (the magnifying glass button). You can then just delete all the emails in the search results.

New Label where you can input the new name. Choose the label you want, **Jobs** in this example, (once it is created) and click on the box next to **Also apply filter to x matching conversations** before clicking on **Create filter**. This will then apply to all old emails already in your account and new email that you will receive in the future.

Setting up filters from related email in your inbox (Filter messages like these)

There is a quick way of creating filters straight from your inbox. This will save you an enormous amount of time.

1. Check the box next to the emails that you want to filter,

2. Click on **More**,

3. Select **Filter messages like these**:

Gmail will populate the From field for you so any action you choose on the next screen will apply to any messages sent from the email addresses of the emails you originally selected.

4. On the bottom right of the pop-up choose **Create filter with this search**

5. Choose what you want done with these type of emails. It will apply to all emails from that address. You can label, filter or even delete as soon as they come in

6. If you want the action to apply to your existing emails, check the box next to **Also apply filter to x matching conversations**

7. Click on **Create filter**

Unsubscribe from unwanted newsletters

You may have signed up to newsletters in the past that you may no longer want. You can unsubscribe manually using the instructions at the bottom of emails. This is not always a reliable method as there are some disreputable companies that don't always unsubscribe you.

If you definitely did not sign up to the email and there are no unsubscribe links in the email, click on the spam button at the top of the email.

FIGURE 12.6 Report spam to Google by clicking on this button.

12

Chapter summary

People can only ever give you advice on how to deal with your email. Organizing your email is a highly personal thing. What works for you does not necessarily work for someone else. You may prefer to have all your emails in a subject together as a discussion while another may want to turn this feature off (possible in Gmail) and have each email come in separately so you can see instantly what needs to be done.

It is possible you do not receive many emails at all, in which case I am very jealous, but this does make much of this chapter irrelevant. Maybe all you need is the Google inbox tabs or you are happy to turn them off and deal with emails as they come in. There is no correct way to deal with email only what works for you.

Organising your email is a continual process, using the **Filter messages like these** option will make this easier but there will always be the odd email which doesn't fit into any category. Unsubscribing and the spam button are also important tools in your fight to keep your emails under control.

Using all of the tips in this chapter will not only save you time but will make you work more efficiently.

Chapter 13

Chat

What to expect in this chapter:

- Turning on Chat

- Inviting contacts to chat

- Video, phone or text chat

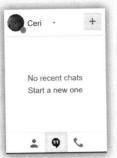

FIGURE 13.1 Chat is located at the bottom left of the Gmail homepage.

Gmail gives you the option to chat to your contacts. Chat has changed over the years and the new chat is based on Google Hangouts. The name may change over time to reflect this, so if Chat does disappear from your settings, it may have changed its name to Hangouts.

Sometimes you might want to get an answer quickly and if you see that your contact is online, it can be faster to open a text or video chat rather than send an email and wait for a response. If Chat is not visible at the bottom of the left navigation pane on the Gmail homepage you will need to turn on Chat first from the settings.

Turning on Chat

The Chat function can be found in the left navigation bar on your Gmail homepage. You will need to invite someone to chat in the first instance but after that, your contact will be in the chat list.

1. Go to the **gear wheel** at the top right of the screen, this is the main settings button
2. Click on **Settings**
3. On the top row, select **Chat**
4. Turn chat on by choosing **Chat on**
5. Click **Save Changes** at the bottom of the screen

FIGURE 13.2 Invite your contact to be able to chat with them.

Inviting a contact to chat

The chat section of Gmail is on the bottom left of the Gmail screen, always available even when you are typing emails. If you can't see Chat and you know it is enabled, click on the speech button with the quotation marks inside to open the section.

To add a contact, click on the person symbol at the bottom of the screen (the first button). Either click on **Find someone** or the button with the plus sign on it which is beside your profile picture in the chat section.

Type your contact's name, email address or phone number in the search box. Google will look through your contacts in your Gmail account or contact them through the email address.

Before you can contact the person, they will be notified that you are trying to contact them for the first time. They will have to allow this before you can start chatting.

Chat Overview

FIGURE 13.3 Find your invites by clicking on the speech button.

When you click on your contact's name in the chat section of the left navigation bar a pop up will appear on the right of your browser window as you can see from the next image.

To start a text chat, start typing in the box at the bottom (see *figure 13.4*). You can add emoticons by clicking on the smiley face to the left of the box.

Attach an image by clicking on the square on the right of the box. When you hover over the image you get a second image of a pencil to its left. This allows you to 'draw' an image and send it.

Above the conversation, you can click on the video camera icon to start a video call.

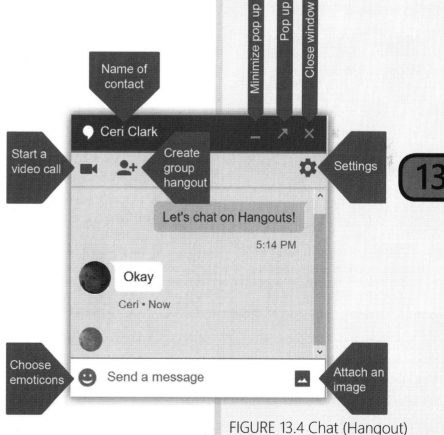

FIGURE 13.4 Chat (Hangout) overview in Gmail.

To chat to more than one person, select the person icon with the plus next to it.

If you want to have the chat in its own browser window, choose the pop out button on the top right, next to the minimize and exit buttons.

Archiving or deleting conversations

If you do not want to use the dense roster option to de-clutter your chat, you may want to archive or delete older conversations.

Deleting or archiving the conversation will only remove it from your own account. Delete the conversation if you want to permanently remove it. Archive the discussion if you want it to be available in searches in Gmail later.

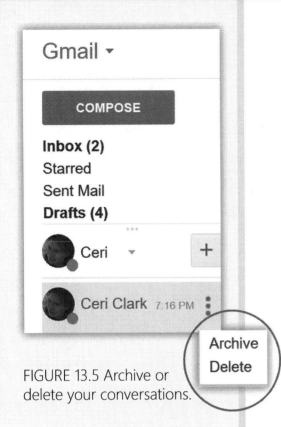

FIGURE 13.5 Archive or delete your conversations.

Searching your Chat history

Using text chat through Gmail does not mean you lose a record of your conversations with your contacts. As long as you do not delete your conversations then they are searchable within Gmail itself at the same time as you search for your emails.

If you find a relevant chat while you are searching your emails, if you click into the discussion, there is a button at the bottom of the conversation marked **Open Hangout**. This will open the chat window and you can resume the conversation.

The contact 'card'

If you hover over your contact's name, the following 'card' will load.

From here you can go straight to your contact's information in Google contacts, see a list of their emails in Gmail as well as contact them through video, text and compose an email to them.

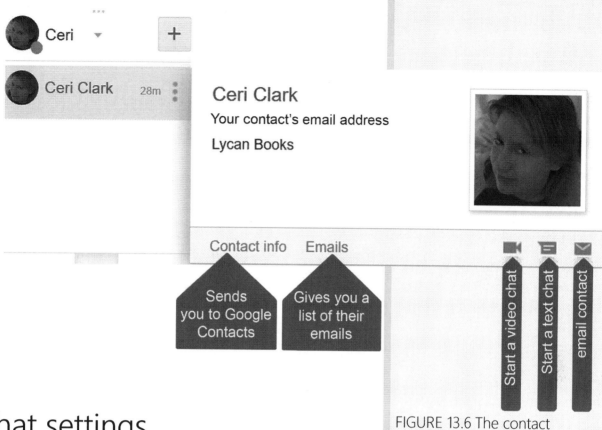

FIGURE 13.6 The contact card.

Chat settings

You can access your global chat settings by clicking the little downwards arrow next to your name and profile picture. *Figure 13.7* shows what options are available.

Global chat settings

Beside your profile picture you can type in a status that you want your contacts to see. This can be busy, away from the desk or even a time frame such as, I will be back in ten minutes.

Directly underneath your status you can allow your contacts to see when you were last active, what device you are on and when you are talking to someone else.

The second option may not be a good idea as it may show you are out and about and not in your office or home. However, this information is only showed to people you are in contact with on Google hangouts so this may not be a problem.

The next options are notifications. This will mute your notifications for a period of time from one hour to one week. You are able to differentiate this option between muting your messages and/or phone calls.

In the **General** section of the settings, you can get Chat/Hangouts to automatically convert any text that you type into picture emojis.

Use dense roster will tidy up your view of chat in the left navigation bar. It will remove avatars and recent messages giving a cleaner, less cluttered look.

Archived Hangouts, **Invites**, **Hidden contacts** and **Blocked People** will allow you to see lists of these on a new 'page'.

Selecting **Recommended** under **Customize invite settings** will allow people who already have your contact details to send you a message directly. If they don't have any way of already contacting you then they must send you an invite. Using the recommended setting could save you from missing a message from a friend or colleague.

Sign out of Hangouts will log you out of Hangouts. You will have to sign back in from Chat in the left navigation bar to be able to contact people using chat in Gmail again.

Conversation specific settings

Within your conversation you can click on the gear wheel/cog to get even more settings.

- Turn **Notifications** on or off for this particular conversation
- See the **Conversation history** for this person.
- **Archive the conversation**
- **Delete the conversation**
- **Block 'X'** (the contact)

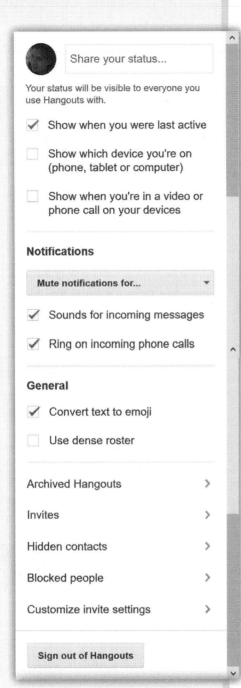

FIGURE 13.7 Chat settings

Blocking contacts

If you would like the option of blocking a person you are chatting to, this could be particularly useful for ex-boyfriends/girlfriends, you can do this by the following method.

Click on **Ignore** at the bottom of the invite, you can then choose to **Report** or **Block** the person contacting you. Click **OK** for this to take affect.

You also do not have to accept invites to connect.

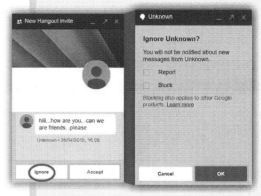

FIGURE 13.8 You can Block a contact by clicking on Ignore on the invite.

Video, phone or text chat

Whether you want to video, phone or text chat depends on the circumstances at the time you are trying to contact them. This could be anything from having a bad hair day, a work from home and forgot accidentally-on-purpose to take off my pyjamas and wear work clothes day or more seriously, the other person is busy and you can type a message and you don't mind waiting for an answer. People will usually respond to chat messages a lot quicker than email.

If you click on the video icon then the hangout window will load. To call click on the phone symbol and to text, just start typing.

Chapter summary

When you need to contact someone in a hurry through text chat or a phone call or you want a more personal way of communicating through a video call, Google's chat provides this through the integration of Google Hangouts into Gmail with the moniker Chat.

You cannot contact anyone without their permission, whether that is through them allowing you to contact them because you already have their phone number or email address or they have accepted your invitation to talk. If you do not want to connect with someone you can block or report them.

Chats can be deleted but if you keep or archive them then they are searched at the same time as your emails. There are numerous settings within chat which can be turned on or off depending on your needs. Chat can be a more immediate way of contacting friends, family or co-workers. You can let people know with the status option if you are busy or available to talk.

Chapter 14

Tasks

What to expect in this chapter:

- Getting the most out of Tasks

- Creating tasks

- Deleting tasks

- Organizing tasks

FIGURE 14.1 Tasks location

Tasks are a great way of remembering lists of things to do. As long as you have access to the internet you can add, edit and delete from your task list wherever you are. Whether on your smartphone or on your computer at home, use tasks to organize your life.

Where to find Tasks

Tasks can be found on the left navigation bar in the top left corner of your screen as seen in *figure 14.1*.

By clicking on **Tasks** a pop up will appear on the bottom right of the screen which looks like *figure 14.2*.

The buttons on the top of the task window do three things:

Button 1: minimizes the window

Button 2: pops the window to a larger, new browser window

Button 3: Closes the Task window

The options on the bottom of the screen are (from left to right)

Button 4: Actions. These include moving tasks in a list, emailing, printing, viewing, sorting and clearing tasks in a list

Button 5: The plus sign adds a new task

Button 6: Clicking on the trash can/bin symbol deletes a task

Button 7: The lists options include refresh, rename, delete and create a new list

Adding a task

To add a task, click next to the little white box and start typing. After you've made the first task you can then click on the + button at the bottom of each window to make another (number 5 in *figure 14.2*).

FIGURE 14.2 Tasks overview

168

Other ways to start a new task

- Pressing enter after you have finished typing a new task will start a new one
- Clicking directly under the last task in the list will also create a new task

If you want to add more details to a task (such as a due date) click on the arrow pointing right, on the line of the subject and the page in the next figure will load:

Click on **Back to List**, and the main tasks window will appear again. All the information is then displayed under the task subject. There is no need to save, Google will automatically do this for you.

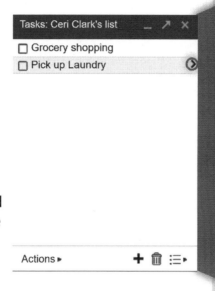

FIGURE 14.3 Adding more details to tasks.

Completing a task

To complete a task simply check the box next to the subject. The text will have a line through it so you know you've done it.

Deleting or removing a task

To remove a task, click on the subject and click on the trash can (bin) symbol at the bottom of the task window.

Actions

Clicking on **Actions** as seen in **figure 14.5** can give you more options.

FIGURE 14.4 Example of a tasks list.

13

Indent and Unindent

These options will allow you to move dependent tasks as if you were using Tab in a word processor. Click on the subject, then **Actions**, then **Indent**. The subject will then move a little to the right. For an example of how this might work see the **figure 14.6**.

Clicking on the indented item and then **Actions** > **Unindent** will send the item back to the left.

Move up or down

Similar to indenting, click on the subject > **Actions** > **Move up/Move down**.

You can also move tasks by hovering over the tasks and 'grabbing' the dots that appear to the left and moving it up or down with your mouse.

Edit details

This option will bring up the details page again. Clicking on the arrow next to each task will do the same thing.

Help

Clicking on this will send you to Google's help pages on using Tasks.

Show tips

This will show you tips in the Tasks window.

Email task list

Have a list which you want your partner or friend to see? Email them the list.

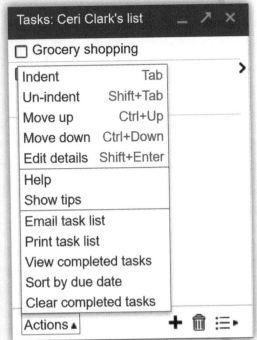

FIGURE 14.5 **Actions available in Tasks**

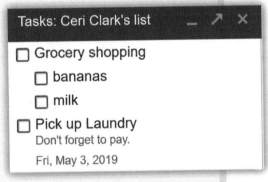

FIGURE 14.6 **Task indenting in action**

Print task list

This sends your list to your printer.

View completed tasks

This is useful if you just want to see what you have completed/organized by date.

Sort by due date

If you have put dates to your tasks, see what you need to complete first.

Clear completed tasks

Just have your uncompleted tasks in your list.

Organizing lists

On the bottom bar of the task window click on the list button (as circled in *figure 14.7*) to bring up some options for creating and editing task lists.

These options are **Refresh list**, **Rename list**, **Delete list**, **New list** and then the lists you have already made.

You can have more than one list, choose the list you want from the bottom of the options that appears when you click on the three lines icon (menu button).

Chapter summary

Tasks are a great way to keep track of life events or general tasks within Gmail. Adding and removing a task is a breeze while the indenting options means that you can categorize these tasks in groups.

Checking the boxes next to your tasks will put lines

FIGURE 14.7 Organize your lists.

13

through them so you know they are completed.

If you want to remind someone of your tasks list, you can email them the list or print it out. Have different lists for different areas of your life.

Chapter 15

Netiquette

What to expect in this chapter:

- Traditions of communicating over the internet

- What to do with trolls

If this is your first email account you may not be familiar with some of the traditions of Netiquette. Here are the top rules of email etiquette.

1. Never type your emails ALL IN CAPS LOCK! IT WILL SEEM TO THE READER THAT YOU ARE SHOUTING AT THEM

2. If you use abbreviations or acronyms, write them out in full during first use. After that you don't need to explain it in the same email

3. Don't remove previous messages from your email thread when replying. The person you are emailing may have deleted your previous emails altogether and if you reply with no history they may have no idea what you are talking about

4. When replying, start your message at the top of the thread. This is so your friends, colleagues and other contacts don't have to scroll down an exceedingly long list just to find out what you have to say

5. If you have a long reply, try to put a summary of the most important items at the beginning of your email. Most people scan-read emails when they are busy and if you want them to do something make sure it is obvious at the beginning of the email

6. Use a meaningful subject. Should I bother to read this email? If it just says "Howdy", the recipient might think it is spam. And at the same time don't send emails with a blank subject either!

7. Don't forward chain-emails, unless it is a really funny one, and you know your friend will appreciate it

8. Read the email before you send it. What sounds perfectly reasonable when you are writing can seem really insulting after ten minutes – and that's when you are not trying to be insulting!

9. Be careful when replying to mailing lists. Remember that email can go to hundreds if not thousands of people

10. Don't make personal remarks about people in jest. The reader can't see the glint in your eye as you are being ironic

11. Don't post your email address on websites unless you want to be sent a lot of spam

12. Be respectful, imagine you are talking to someone you know. Sending an email can seem anonymous, but people's feelings can still be hurt

13. If you don't know the person you are contacting, make an extra effort to make your emails as clear and concise as possible

14. Keep your fonts and language simple. Make sure you do not use yellow, grey or light colors when emailing people. They are difficult to see, why make life hard for people? You may think it looks cool, but if your contact has to highlight, copy it, then paste it into word, change the color and make it bigger to read it, let's just say your email might go unread

15. If someone comments on one of your posts on social networks and it appears malicious, they are most probably a troll. They are posting to get a response. In this situation, ignore them. Nothing annoys a troll more than if they think someone hasn't noticed a comment designed to infuriate

Chapter summary

This is a very short chapter but the information in it can make yours, and your email recipient's life a lot easier. Thinking about the person who will be reading your email can go a long way to getting it read. Saving them time reading it will mean that they are more likely to do so and your hit rate for getting things done will explode.

15

Inbox by Gmail

What to expect in this chapter:

- An overview of Inbox

- How to get to Inbox by Gmail

- Composing and viewing emails, and reminders

- Bundles, what are they and how to use them

- Snoozing and removing emails

- Inbox by Gmail settings

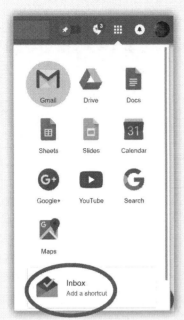

FIGURE 16.1 **Adding the Inbox icon to your app launcher.**

Inbox by Gmail is another way to view and interact with your emails. Your emails are hosted from the same place so if you delete or archive an email from Inbox or Gmail they will be deleted or archived in the other service. Inbox is more about automated organization and Gmail personalized configuration. Choosing whether to use Inbox or Gmail is a choice about your work style. No option is better than the other but allows you to interact with your emails in the way that suits you best.

There is nothing to say that you cannot use the Gmail app or Inbox by Gmail at the same time. You could even use Gmail while you are 'training' Inbox. Alternatively you could use both 'apps' for different situations. In some cases you may need to see and deal with your emails as they come in but at other times, you want bundle your emails and get a larger picture of your work, in which case Inbox could be more suitable in those situations.

Use the main features of bundles, pinning, sweep, and snooze to organize your life.

How to get to Inbox by Gmail

Inbox is available on your computer and your mobile device whether it is a phone or a tablet.

Getting to Inbox from your computer

Type in the following internet address in your browser to go directly there on your computer:

https://www.google.com/inbox

Click on **SIGN IN** on the top right of the screen.

You can also get to Inbox using the App launcher. This is the button with nine squares located on the top right of your browser window when you are on any Google page. It is in the shape of a square as shown in *figure 16.1*.

You can add the Inbox icon to the app launcher and move it to any location within the app launcher.

1. Sign into **Inbox** at https://www.google.com/inbox

2. Click on the button with nine squares located on the top right of your browser window (know as the App launcher or Waffle)

3. Click on **Add to Shortcut** (circled in *figure 16.1*)

4. Grab the Inbox icon with your mouse and drag it up to where you want it to be. In the example in *figure 16.2*, I have put it as the first icon but you can just as easily put it anywhere in the list

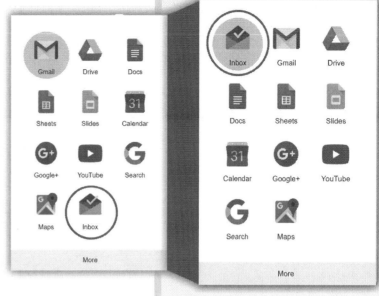

FIGURE 16.2 **Moving the icon in the app launcher.**

Google will remember this and it will appear at the top of every Google page where you are logged in.

Getting to Inbox from your mobile device

Inbox by Gmail is available on Apple's iOS and Android's Gmail as well as on computers. Navigate to your mobile device's app store to download the app. Once you have done this, open **Inbox by Gmail** from your app list.

Getting started

Inbox learns how you want your email to be dealt with over time. However, spending some time setting it up at the beginning can save you a lot of time in the long run.

These instructions are for using the web layout but you can do the same from your mobile apps and there will be notes in this chapter in key areas for how to do actions in the app versions.

Every time you so something in Inbox, the service learns how you work and your experience will improve over time.

179

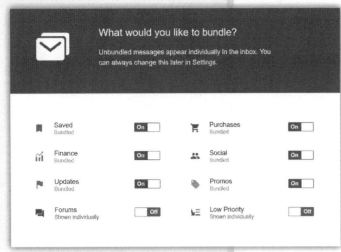

FIGURE 16.3 Setting up your first bundles.

1. Go to Inbox at https://www.google.com/inbox

2. Click on **SIGN IN** on the top right of the screen. A tutorial will load

3. Click on the right arrows until your are given the option to set up your first bundles, *see figure 16.1*

4. Check what Google suggests and click on the arrow to the right if you are happy with the suggestions.

You can change these or any other bundles later in settings.

Inbox overview

The overall look of Inbox is similar to Gmail but there are some key differences, which includes a more uncluttered look.

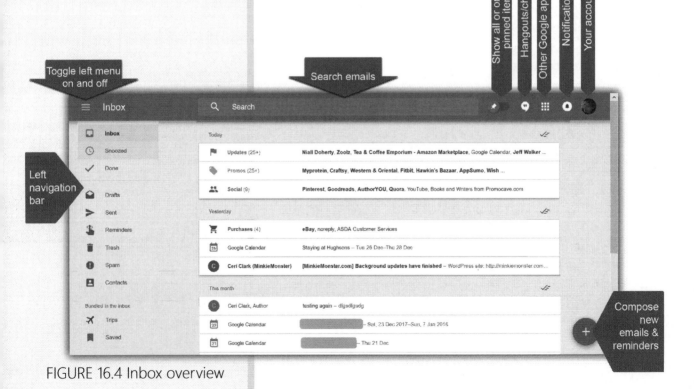

FIGURE 16.4 Inbox overview

Toggle Menu on and off

When you first see Inbox there is no left navigation menu. Click on the three horizontal lines at the top left of the window to see it.

Search emails

As with the Gmail website, search your emails by typing in this box. The advanced search options are not available in Inbox.

Show all or only pinned items

You can pin items to keep them at the top of your inbox but also to keep them while you do a sweep.

Hangouts/chat

View or create new chat messages through the integrated Google Hangouts.

App launcher (Other Google apps)

When you press on the squares (on the top right of your screen), you will be given the option to go to other Google services like Docs, Slides, Drive and Maps etc. You can add more apps to the initial list and re-arrange them as you prefer them laid out. For example, you may use Inbox and Docs more than any other Google service. The icons can be moved around so they appear at the top.

Notifications

These are Google+ notifications. You can safely ignore these if you have no intention of joining Google+.

16

Your Account

Here you can change your account options, find out about Google's privacy policy and update your Google settings. This is where you can add or change your profile picture and manage your security settings for Google.

Left navigation menu

There are a few options in this navigation menu, here is a quick breakdown of what is possible from here.

Inbox: Click on Inbox to get to the Inbox homepage from anywhere in this website, including your bundles.

Snoozed: Click on this to find any items you have snoozed quickly.

Done: This will take you to items you have declared as done as well as archived items.

Drafts: If you started to write a message but never finished or sent it, you can find it here.

Sent: Look here for emails you have sent out.

Reminders: If you have created any reminders, this is the place to look for them.

Trash or Bin: If you delete emails then they don't disappear. They will be in the Trash/Bin folder for 30 days. Click on **EMPTY TRASH** (or **BIN** in the UK) **NOW**, to remove the emails permanently in one go.

Spam: Anything Google deems spam will appear in here. You can train Gmail to recognise any spam that you get in your inbox (but they've missed) by marking it as spam manually.

Contacts: Clicking on this will open Google Contacts in a new window.

Bundled in the inbox: Your bundled emails under 'labels' will go here. Click on the bundle and the emails will load in the main window. To get out of this view, click on the inbox at the top of the menu.

Unbundled: The links here can lead to emails from labels created in Gmail (as opposed to Inbox). You will find a link to **Low Priority** emails here that Google feels you are less likely to read.

Create new...: Make a new bundle and choose which email addresses get bundles in it and/or other information.

Settings: You can change how you interact with Inbox from here. I will go into more detail further in this chapter.

Help & Feedback: View Google's own help pages and let them know what you think of Inbox from this link.

Compose emails and reminders

The red button with the plus button will allow you to compose new emails but also new reminders. People that you regularly contact will also appear directly above the button to save you time when replying to them.

Composing emails and reminders button

As with the main Gmail website, click on the button with the plus on it on the bottom right corner of your browser. The key difference here is that you can set reminders with this button as well as view regular contacts for more efficient emailing.

On your mobile device, press in the red circle with a plus on it and then you can press on the pencil to compose a new message, the hand to make a new reminder or press on one of your contacts to speed up the email creation process.

Bundles

Bundles will sort all types of emails into one group so that you can see all similar emails together. This can be

FIGURE 16.5 Filter your messages so that are bundled by email address, subject or keyword.

useful to keep all your emails from your friends, family, colleagues, projects and even events together. You will have to create and manually organize them to begin with but over time, Inbox will learn what you want bundled. This is similar to labels in Gmail but relies on automation to filter the emails for you over time. If you have created labels in Gmail, these will appear in the left navigation menu. Please note that you cannot create a bundle name that is the same as a label you have already created. You can only put an email into one bundle unlike labels where you can have one email in many labels.

Creating Bundles

1. Towards the bottom of the left navigation menu, look for **+Create new...**
2. Type in a descriptive name and click on **SAVE**
3. Click on **ADD**
4. Choose how you want Google to add emails to the bundle. This could be from their email address (**From**), who you send the email to (**To**), what you or your contact puts in the subject line (**Subject**), emails that include certain keywords (**Includes**) and finally emails that don't include certain words (**Excludes**)

There are only two boxes to start with but as you type in the second, a third will appear and so on until you have the combination that is right for you.

The process is the same on your mobile device. Press the three horizontal lines button on the top left of your app to get the left menu. Choose **+Create new** and follow the instructions above.

Moving your email into Bundles

FIGURE 16.6 Menu button for moving your emails into bundles.

You can move your emails into your bundles from two places by clicking on the button with three vertical dots (**Move to**). First hover over your email and click on the **Move to** button or click on the check box that appears when you hover over your contact's profile picture, flag, reminder or calendar icon. In this case, the **Move to** button will appear at the top of the screen.

Click on the bundle you want to move it to and you will have 8 seconds to click on **Undo the move** that will appear on the bottom left of your screen.

It will move from your inbox. If you want to find it again, go into the bundle you moved it into, in the left menu.

If you want to remove your email from a bundle, click on the **Move to** button, as above, again but this time, choose **Remove from** [Your Bundle Name].

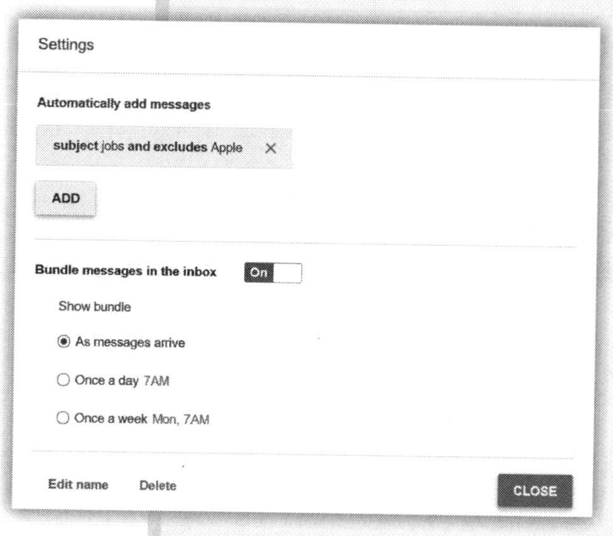

Bundle settings

When you are in a bundle or you hover your mouse over the bundle name in the left menu, you should see a cog or gear wheel symbol. The bundle settings are accessed from here.

The Settings pop up will allow you to do three things.

1. Add criteria to your bundle that will send emails to this bundle

2. Snooze your bundle so that you don't have to see it every day. If you have a newsletters bundle for example, you could have it appear once a week at the end of the day on Friday. This could act as a reminder that it is nearly time to go home but also a reminder to keep abreast of developments in your field

3. Edit the name of your bundle. If a project changes its name, click on **Edit name** at the bottom left of the settings page and change it to reflect the new title

Pinning

Pinning your emails or reminders can make them easier to find and can enable a clean sweep of the inbox. You can

FIGURE 16.7 Settings available for your bundle.

16

FIGURE 16.8 Delete the email by clicking on the trash can (bin) symbol.

FIGURE 16.9 The tick symbol will mark your items as Done.

FIGURE 16.10 The Sweep symbol.

completely declutter the look and see what is important by toggling the pin button on the top of the screen as illustrated in *figure 16.4*. This will mean that you only see what you have designated as important and when you want to see the rest of the email just toggle the button again and everything will appear again.

Clear that email

There are several way of clearing your inbox of your emails, reminders and calendar items. You could mark them as done, delete the emails or sweep a number of them away at the same time. A word of warning: if you delete an email from Inbox then it will be deleted from Gmail as well. If you can't find an email or reminder and you know you haven't deleted it, then there is always the option of firing up Gmail and looking in **All Mail**.

Deleting email

Deleted emails will still be in your trash (bin in the UK) for 30 days after you delete it. This will be the same in Gmail and Inbox. Any emails in your trash will not be searchable. To delete your item, click on the trash symbol.

Done

Mark your items as **Done** (tick symbol) to archive them. They will be removed from your inbox but will still be searchable. You can also find them in **Done** from the left menu. If you are looking for the emails in Gmail itself, they will be in **All Mail**.

Sweep it away

Use **Sweep** with **Pinning** to remove all your unwanted email from your inbox in one go. How this works is that if you pin all your important emails then you can sweep and all other emails in your inbox or bundle will be archived. The only way to find those emails in Inbox after a Sweep is if you search for them.

Above the date you want to sweep, look for the **sweep** icon as shown in *figure 16.10*. Clicking on the sweep button will archive everything that has not been pinned in the time frame you have chosen. If you want to just get rid of a bundle, click on the **Done** icon as seen in *figure 16.9*.

Viewing your emails

Click on your email to view it, If they are in a bundle, click on the bundle and it will expand so that you can select individual emails within them. This process is the same on your computer and mobile device.

Snooze

The Snooze feature in Inbox allows you to send an email away until you need to see or do something with it. You can even have it so that the email you want to snooze comes back repeatedly until you stop it. If you want to find your snoozed emails and it isn't back yet, just find the **Snooze** link in the left menu. Press on the menu button (three horizontal lines) to see it on your mobile app.

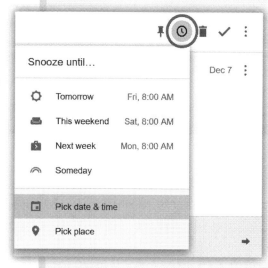

FIGURE 16.11 Snooze your items to temporarily remove them from your inbox.

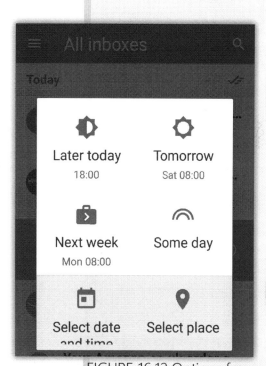

1. On your email click on the clock symbol
2. Select a time or click on **Pick date & time**
3. You will need to pick a date and time
4. Click on the little arrow next to **Does not repeat**
5. Choose **Daily**, **Weekly**, **Monthly** or **Yearly** or a custom time period such as every week on a Wednesday by selecting **Custom**
6. Choose an end time if you want one
7. Click on **SAVE**

On your mobile device, swipe your email or reminder left to snooze it.

FIGURE 16.12 Options for snoozing length in the Inbox app.

You will get the choice to snooze it to **Later today,**

16

FIGURE 16.13 Hover over the plus button and it will change to a pencil and the reminder button will appear above it.

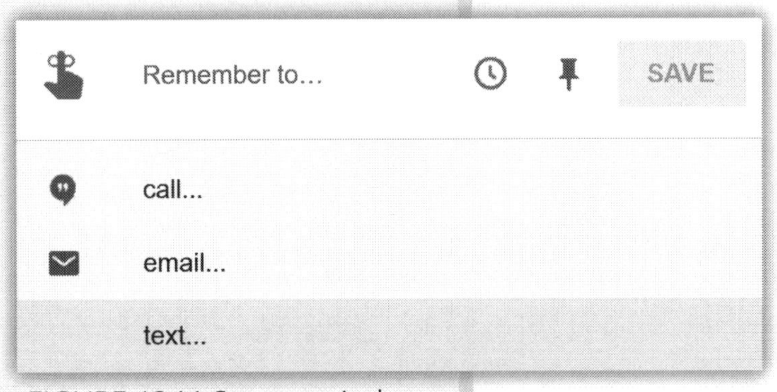

FIGURE 16.14 Set a reminder for a call, email or text.

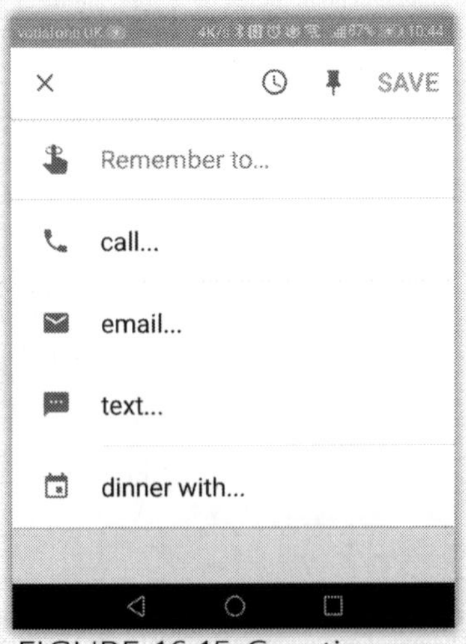

FIGURE 16.15 Creating a reminder in the Inbox app.

tomorrow, next week, some day and you can select a particular date and time as well as place. The app will confirm that the email or reminder has been snoozed. Press on **Undo** and the snooze will be cancelled.

Reminders

Reminders are what sets Inbox by Gmail apart from the main Gmail service. It is easy to create reminders by themselves, from an email or even repeating reminders. You spend so much time in your email every day that including your to-do list as part of the service just makes sense.

Creating Reminders

1. At the bottom right of the window, hover over the red button with the plus (it will change to a pencil as you hover over it) and click on the reminder button

2. You will have the choice to create a reminder for a call, email or text. You can also choose whether to snooze it (the clock icon) or pin it

3. Click on **SAVE**

You can type anything where it says **Remember to** but the call, email and text options are there to speed up the reminder creation. Click on **call** and Google will suggest people you might want to call and reasons for why you might want to call them. Instead of typing call Dad for his birthday, you just need to click three times on Google's suggestions.

On your mobile device press on the red 'plus' button and the process will be the same as for a computer.

Pressing on the call, email, text dinner with, will save you time typing out the message using your keyboard but if you want to type it manually, press on **Remember to** and fill in your reminder information.

Press on the clock icon at the top of the window to choose

a time when you want to be reminded to do this. It will be in your inbox but use the snooze function if you want to be reminded at a certain time.

Creating Reminders from an email

In an open email you can click on the pin symbol to create a reminder.

Start typing next to the hand icon. Remember to click **SAVE** which will appear as soon as you start typing.

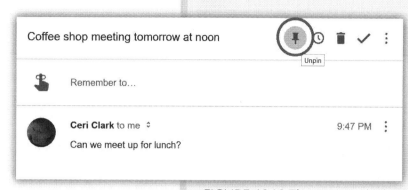

FIGURE 16.16 The pin symbol (circled above) will allow you to set a reminder in an email.

Next to the pin icon, click on the clock to snooze it until you need to see it.

On your mobile device, open the email, press on the pin symbol and start typing. As with your computer *save it* and *snooze it* as needed.

Creating repeated reminders

Follow the steps below to create repeated reminders.

1. At the bottom right of the window, hover over the red button with the plus on (it will change to a pencil as you hover over it) and click on the reminder button

2. Click on **Reminders** in the left menu

3. Hover your mouse over the reminder you want to repeat and click on the clock symbol (snooze)

4. Click on **Pick date & time**

5. You will need to pick a date and time. Please see *figure 16.17* for the options

6. Click on the little arrow next to **Does not repeat**

7. Choose **Daily**, **Weekly**, **Monthly** or **Yearly** or a custom time period such as every week on a Wednesday by selecting **Custom**

16

189

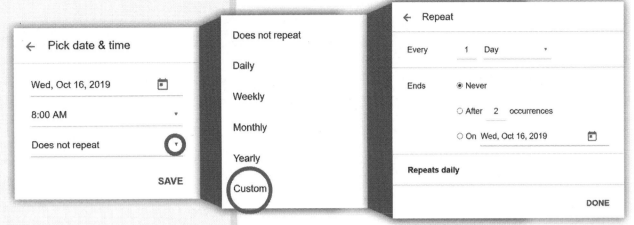

FIGURE 16.17 Creating repeated reminders.

8. Choose an end time if you want one

9. Click on **SAVE**

On your mobile device the process is similar.

1. Click on the Menu button (three horizontal lines) and choose **Reminders** from the list

2. Press on the reminders you want to repeat

3. Press on the clock symbol

4. Click on **Select date & time**

5. Set an initial date and time

6. Press on **Doesn't repeat** choose how often you want it to repeat

7. Click **SAVE**

Viewing reminders

If your reminders are not in your inbox, check the reminders link in the left navigation menu.

The Inbox settings

The inbox settings are very similar on your computer as on your mobile device. You can find them on the left menu. However, when removing a message you can choose whether to mark them as done or delete them on the app. There is also the option for an out of office message (in the signature settings) on the app which does not appear on the computer settings.

Labels

These labels are your bundles. You can get to the bundle specific settings by clicking on the gear wheel that appears when you hover over the label/bundle. Take a look at *Bundle settings* for more information on what you can do with these settings.

Signature

Toggle the on button in **Signature** to create some text that will appear at the end of your emails. There are no formatting options in Inbox at the time of writing. Using templates could be a way around this.

Out of Office (only in the mobile app)

Press on the **Out of Office** option. See **figure 16.18** to see how it looks on the app. Toggle the button at the top to turn it on and choose your first and last days. Remember to press on **Send to my contacts only**. Anyone can send you an email and get your message otherwise and you might not want to tell burglars that you will be away for a while.

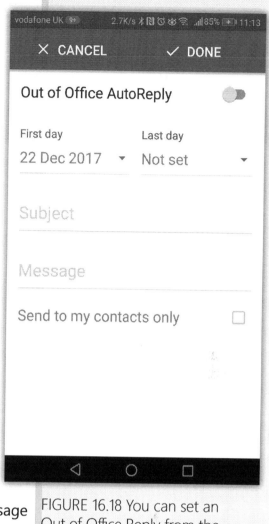

FIGURE 16.18 You can set an Out of Office Reply from the mobile Inbox app.

Notifications (on the mobile app)

Change how you want to be notified of changes to your Inbox from here.

Snooze

You can choose when in the morning, afternoon and evening you want anything snoozed in these time periods to arrive. This just means you could click on morning and you know that your emails will reappear at 9am for example if this is what you set for the morning. You can also set your weekend snooze period.

Assists

Check the boxes in this section if you want Google to give you suggestions about your inbox. This could be for emails that you have forgotten to reply to or suggestions for following up on emails.

Templates

If you have used canned responses in Gmail, they will appear in **Templates** in Inbox.

Create a new template

FIGURE 16.19 Creating a new template.

1. Click on **Settings** on the bottom left of the left menu
2. Click on **Templates**
3. Click on **CREATE A TEMPLATE**
4. Fill in the email. Your subject will be the title of your template
5. Format as desired
6. Click on **CREATE**

Using your template

FIGURE 16.20 Using your templates.

Once you have created your templates or you want to use *Canned responses* that you created in Gmail, you will need to add them to emails you compose.

1. Open a new email
2. Click on the little arrow to the left of the trash can (no. 1 as seen in *figure 16.20*)
3. Click on the Template icon as seen marked as no. 2 in *figure 16.7*
4. Select your template
5. Add the missing information including Subject
6. Check there is no missing information
7. Click on **SEND**

Other

The settings for **other** include adding the ability to use keyboard shortcuts and redirecting Gmail to inbox.google. com. If you do this, you will not be able to use the other Gmail view. You can get to Inbox direct from the URL or using the App launcher that is available on other Google pages. If you do check this box then it can easily be undone by revisiting the settings page and unchecking the box.

A useful feature is to make notifications stay longer on your screen. Eight seconds is not long and you can extend it to a total of 30 seconds by clicking next to this option.

Location settings (only on your mobile device)

Have you ever wanted to be reminded of something as soon as you get to work or there is something you just have to remember when you get home? The location settings in the Inbox app means that you can set up reminders based on where you will be not just a time.

You will have to allow the app to know your location to use this feature. Toggle the button next to **Access my location** to turn it on.

Save your attachments to Drive

Using Drive can keep all your attachments in one place while you can clear your inbox and delete emails. This won't save you any space. Your space is spread across all Google services. It doesn't matter if the 1 GB file in is Gmail or Drive, it will still count to your total. They may be different services but they are all in your one account. You will need to convert the attachments to Google formats to save space. Still you may want to keep all your documents for a project in one place. In this instance saving your attachments in Drive makes sense.

16

1. Hover over the attachment until you see the Google Drive 'triangle' symbol
2. Click on **Save to Drive**
3. Add the file to an existing folder or create a new one
4. Click on **Move**

To save attachments on your mobile device, press on the attachment and press on the triangle Google Drive symbol at the top of your screen. Choose what folder you want the file to be put in and click on **SAVE**.

Chapter summary

Inbox is another way of viewing your emails from Google. What happens in Inbox is reflected in Gmail and vice-versa. You can choose to use one or both of these views and in fact one may be better suited for different ways of working.

Inbox is better for automations and the ability to snooze and sweep your emails. If you want to have a clear out of your emails then using Inbox to do this may be the way to go. However if you want finer control of your email, clearing out your inbox using **Filter messages like these** in Gmail will give you this.

Reminders make Inbox more of an organizational tool. While you can use Calendar to do a similar task, if you spend a lot of time looking at your emails, it makes sense to put your reminders and email in one place.

Templates and Canned messages are interchangeable but the name they have chosen for Inbox (templates) does make more sense and seems more professional. The signature however is not as good as with Gmail.

Both Inbox and Gmail have their advantages and commensurate disadvantages. The choice to use one or the other depends on how you work and that may differ. My advice would be to use both for a while and see which suits you better. There is no rule to say you have to use one so you may end up using both views but at different times.

Chapter 17

Gmail on Your Mobile Phone

What to expect in this chapter:

- An overview of the Gmail app

- Reading and writing emails on your Android device

- Searching your emails

- A look at the settings

With an ever growing number of new smartphones and tablets available there is no excuse to be without your email. Gmail is so simple to set up with an Android device. At the time of writing this book I have a Huawei Mate 9 so these instructions are designed with that phone in mind but the instructions should be similar across all Android phones and tablets.

Gmail should already be installed on your Android device. Browse your Apps list and find the (envelope) icon for Gmail. Your account will have already been set up when you set your Google account on your phone. The screen when you launch the app will look like *figure 17.1*.

Overview

The homepage is deceptively simple. Direct from this page you can view your emails, compose new ones and press on the magnifying glass to search. You can get to everything else including your settings through the Gmail menu.

The Gmail menu

Tapping on the three horizontal lines will take you to the main Gmail menu. In this section you will find:

Switch accounts Click on the circles with profile photos to switch between your accounts. If you press on the arrow directly under these, you will be able to add more accounts, switch between them and manage them.

View emails from all your accounts Press on **All inboxes** to see all your emails from all your accounts in one big list.

Go into your other inboxes The largest profile picture will show which account you are in. Everything under **All inboxes** is from the account you have chosen to view. Therefore if you have an email address called dave@mailinator.com and davesmith@mailinator.com if you have selected the first email address and the profile picture appears first, all the emails in the Primary 'tab'

196

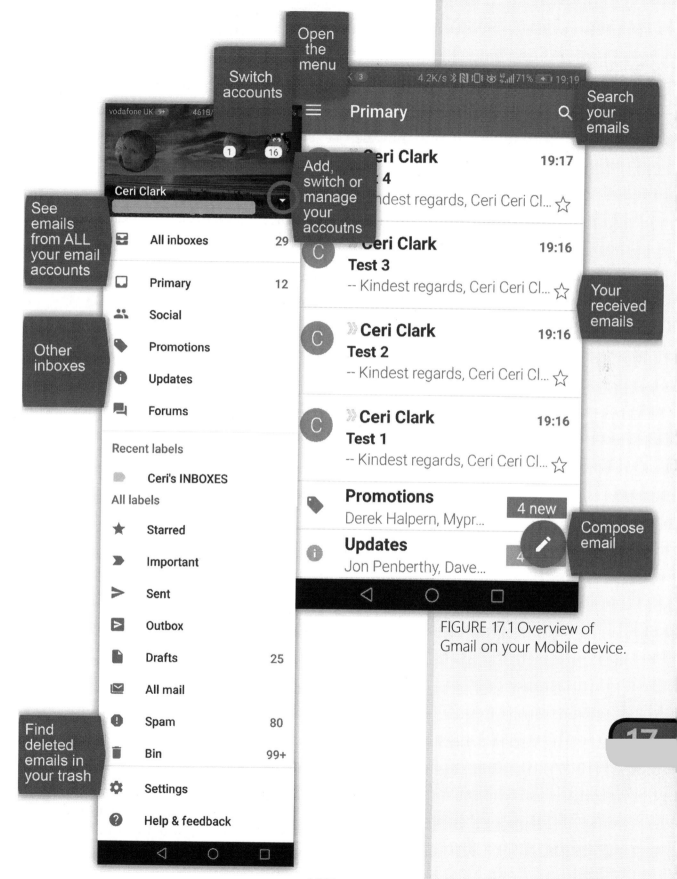

Switch accounts

Open the menu

Search your emails

Add, switch or manage your accoutns

See emails from ALL your email accounts

Other inboxes

Find deleted emails in your trash

Your received emails

Compose email

vodafone UK 9+ 461B/

Ceri Clark

☑	All inboxes	29
☐	Primary	12
☷	Social	
🏷	Promotions	
ⓘ	Updates	
💬	Forums	

Recent labels

▭ Ceri's INBOXES

All labels

★	Starred	
➤	Important	
➢	Sent	
▣	Outbox	
▤	Drafts	25
✉	All mail	
❶	Spam	80
🗑	Bin	99+
⚙	Settings	
❓	Help & feedback	

Primary 🔍

Ceri Clark   19:17
4
-- ...ndest regards, Ceri Ceri Cl... ☆

Ceri Clark   19:16
Test 3
-- Kindest regards, Ceri Ceri Cl... ☆

»**Ceri Clark**   19:16
Test 2
-- Kindest regards, Ceri Ceri Cl... ☆

»**Ceri Clark**   19:16
Test 1
-- Kindest regards, Ceri Ceri Cl... ☆

🏷 **Promotions**
Derek Halpern, Mypr...   4 new

ⓘ **Updates**
Jon Penberthy, Dave...

FIGURE 17.1 Overview of Gmail on your Mobile device.

197

will be from that account. If you want to see all the emails from both accounts together, select **All inboxes**.

Recent labels The labels you last looked at will appear in this section. This saves you hunting through your label list for your most used 'folders'.

All labels Labels included here are, **Starred**, **Important**, **Sent**, **Outbox**, **Drafts**, **All mail**, **Spam** and **Bin/Trash**. If you can't find an email and you know you have not deleted it, look in **All mail**.

Settings Your settings can affect all your Gmail account not just how you view them on your mobile. Take a look at the Android settings section for more information on these.

Help & feedback Take a look at Google's own help pages here or give them feedback on their service.

The email window

Your emails will be displayed in the order Gmail received them and notifications will appear every now and again to let you know if any new email has arrived in your other inboxes (if they are activated). In the screenshot in figure 17.1, *Promotions* and *Updates* inboxes are at the bottom of the screen. When a new email arrives in one of the other inboxes, the notification jumps to the top of the screen with the total amount of unread emails in the 'bar'. When a new email from the *Primary* inbox arrives it will appear above the other inbox emails, unless of course you get another email in one of your other inboxes and so on. This means your latest messages will always be at the top.

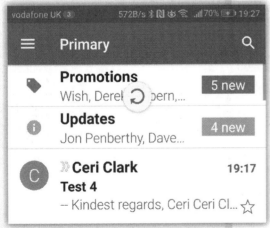

FIGURE 17.2 Refreshing the email list.

Checking mail in the Gmail app

If your phone hasn't synced, press on your phone's screen and draw your finger down. A circling arrow will appear near the top of the screen to let you that Gmail is checking for new messages.

198

Composing mail in the Gmail app

1. Tap on the pen symbol in the circle located on the bottom right of your device's screen

2. Tap on **To** (the email address you are sending from will appear at the top. You can choose a different one if you have set more than one up in your phone's account options)

3. Type in the first few letters, if you have already sent an email to that person from your phone before, Gmail will suggest a person below where you are typing. Select the person by tapping on them

4. Add a subject

5. Type your message

6. (Optional) Press on the paper clip symbol to attach a file from your phone)

7. Tap on the arrow at the top right of the screen to send it

Replying to and forwarding mail in the Gmail app

The arrow pointing left will allow you to reply to an email.

1. Open an email

2. Press on the arrow pointing left (circled in *figure 17.3*) on the right of the screen beside your contact's name and fill in the boxes as necessary

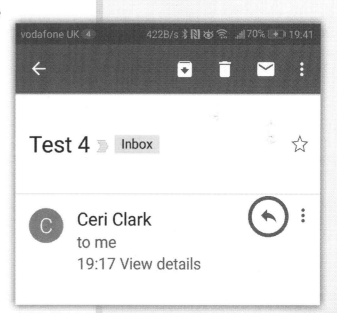

FIGURE 17.3 Press on the arrow to reply.

17

Clicking on the three vertical dots will give you the option to **Reply all**, **Forward**, **Add** or **Remove star**, **Print** (the message) and **Block** the person sending you the message.

199

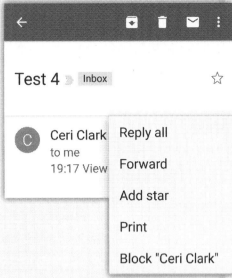

FIGURE 17.4 **Press the three vertical dots for more options.**

Browsing your email using Labels

1. Tap on the top left of the Gmail app (three white lines)
2. Scroll down to the label you want
3. Tap the Label you want to go in

Search your email

1. Tap on the magnifying glass on the top right of the screen
2. Type in your search term and tap on the magnifying glass on your keyboard (or return depending on your keyboard). You will get a list of emails with the search words in them. For tips on searching Gmail please see *Chapter 9 Searching For, and In, Emails*

Settings

You can get to the settings by tapping on the three lines button on the top left of the main screen.

In the top right of the screen there is the three vertical dots menu button. Here you can **Manage Accounts** (takes you to your phone's settings) or you can access **Help & feedback**.

General settings

There are several settings within this section which, once set, will apply to all your Gmail accounts that you use with the Gmail app.

Below is a closer look at the options in the main window but you can get a couple more by clicking on the menu button (three vertical dots). These options are:

Under the menu button in Settings

Manage accounts

This takes you to your phone's settings.

Clear search history

Clears your search record.

Clear picture approval

Stops pictures showing in your emails which you may have approved previously. This will stop all pictures showing automatically so you would have to go and approve them all again if you just wanted to stop getting pictures from one sender!

Help & feedback

Access help from Gmail and provide feedback on their service.

Gmail default action (Archive and delete options)

This setting will determine if your email will be deleted when you swipe or archived. I always choose archive as it is easier to find the emails if they are mistakenly archived than if they are deleted.

Conversation view

If you are using IMAP, POP3 or an Exchange account, you can group emails within conversations. This is great for keeping related emails together.

17

Swipe actions

This is a great time saver. If this setting is activated, swipe your finger to the left or right on the email you want to archive or delete depending on how you set the previous option and it will go. You will have the option to undo for a couple of seconds if you made the gesture by mistake.

Sender image

If you have this setting on, you will see the picture of the sender of the email in the information when you are browsing your emails. If you turn it off you will be able to see more of the message on the home screen as it will expand to fill the space the picture took up.

Default reply action

This option will allow you to choose **Reply** or **Reply all** as a standard action when you press on the arrow to reply.

I do not recommend that you have this setting on. Replying to all is very dangerous if you are in a hurry. The email may go to people you do not intend it to. You can always choose to Reply all to each message as you reply, but having a blanket settings could cause problems.

Auto-fit messages

If you have messages that don't wrap easily, this option will shrink it so it fits in the window. You can then zoom in to read the text.

Auto-advance

When you archive or delete you can choose here whether you want to go to a newer or older message or go to the conversation list.

Action confirmations

- Confirm before deleting
- Confirm before archiving
- Confirm before sending

These options are self-explanatory. If you want Gmail to ask whether you are sure that you want to delete, archive or send your message then turning this on will help you.

Email settings

These settings apply to the email address you specify.

My account

Click here to manage your Google account from your mobile device. The four options here are:

- Update your profile photo.
- Sign-in & Security
- Personal info & privacy
- Account preferences

These are your Google settings and apply to all Google services from Calendar, Drive to Google+.

For more information on *Sign-in and Security*, take a look at *Chapter 4 Security*. This is where you can change your password and manage your other security options.

The personal info section is for what you want shared with the world. You can also see who you've blocked, if you are sharing your location and where you can manage your Google activity. For some of these settings you will be redirected to a browser on your mobile device. I would advice that you use a computer when changing these important settings.

Your account preferences include payments for Google products. This could be the app store or if you have subscriptions through Google Play.

17

Other information in this section include what language you have chosen for your account, How much storage you have in your Google account, deleting Google services like Gmail. To delete Google services you will be redirected to the internet which is a good idea as you don't want to press on this by accident!

More general settings (on an email account basis)

Inbox type

By choosing this option you can make the *Priority inbox* your default inbox. I would recommend you do this only after a couple of months of using your email and you are sure that Google is tagging the right emails as important.

Inbox categories

This is where you choose which inboxes you want the emails to be filtered by in your Gmail. These are **Primary**, **Social**, **Promotions**, **Updates** and **Forums**. You can also drag all your starred emails in to the primary inbox here as well no matter how old they are.

Notifications and Inbox sound & vibrate

Control if and how you get notifications with this setting.

Signature

The Signature you created on the web version of Gmail does not apply on your smartphone. You must create another one here. There are no formatting options for your signature on the mobile version of Gmail.

Smart reply

Gmail will suggest replies when it can if you have this turned on. It can save you time.

Vacation responder/Out of office auto-reply

You can set up a vacation/holiday responder here. If you do set one up I would advise that you check the button for it to work with your contacts only. Burglars have been known to break into houses when they know the owners are on their vacation/holiday.

Sync Gmail and days of mail to sync

If you are going to use this app, you need to sync your Gmail but you can choose how many of those emails you want on your phone by choosing how many days of your messages you want on there.

Manage labels

This is where you can turn on syncing for individual labels. It is not for creating/editing or deleting labels.

Download attachments

Choose whether you want attachments to be auto-downloaded.

Images

This is where you can get Gmail to ask before showing you images in your email or to always show them. It is best to have the setting on **Ask before showing**. There are a couple of possible reasons for this:

1. A spammer can use an image to see if your address is real. When you open an email, images are drawn

from across the web. Spammers can record that it has been seen. The spammer can then sell your email or try to send emails to him/herself knowing that there is a possibility the spam message could be read.

2. Another reason could be that in the past viruses were hidden within images. This has for the most part been stopped as Google will block those they know about and spammers/hackers have now moved on to other means of harm or easier targets but there is still the possibility. If you only allow images to be shown from trusted sources then this threat is pretty much eliminated.

Adding another email account

You can add an account in two places; the first is by pressing on the menu button on the top left of the screen on the main window (your main email list) and then pressing on your face or email address, or you can go to **Settings** and press on **Add account**.

In each location you will be given the option to choose Google, a Gmail address or Personal (IMAP/POP), Yahoo, outlook etc. In each case follow the on screen instructions.

Chapter summary

Over the years the Gmail app has become more versatile. You can do a lot with the app but there are still limitations where you are redirected to the website. This is a good thing as it is easy to press a button by accident on a touch screen and losing access to emails, files and everything else on a Google account would be disastrous if it wasn't done this way.

This chapter gives an overview of the Gmail app, how to compose emails, where Gmail has placed your labels and where and what the settings are. When you are not at your desktop or laptop, Gmail on your mobile device has everything you need.

Chapter 18

Gmail Labs

What to expect in this chapter:

- What are Labs

- What can you do with Gmail using Labs

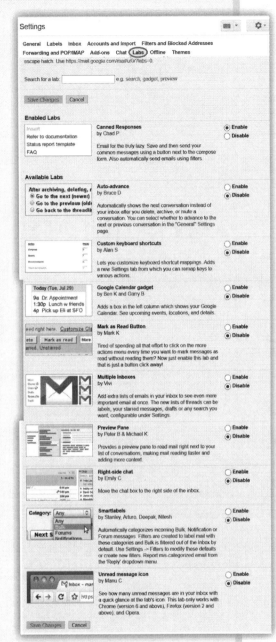

FIGURE 18.1 Labs available.

Google Labs are experimental features that Google are testing. They may disappear at any time or if they become popular, appear as standard options later. I'm going to go through the labs that are available. To find the labs, click on the gear wheel at the top right of Gmail and then go to **Settings** > **Labs**.

Auto-advance

This lab is great for busy Gmailers. If you are tired of going back to the inbox just to get to the next email then enabling this lab will mean you automatically go to it after you delete, archive or mute the email you are reading. When it is enabled you can choose whether to go to an earlier or later conversation.

Canned Responses

Canned responses can save you time by automating your email. Please see *Chapter 12 Email management* for more information.

Custom keyboard shortcuts

Change or make your own keyboard shortcuts, simply enable this lab (clicking save changes at the bottom of the page) and then go to **Gear wheel** > **Settings** > **Keyboard Shortcuts**. The new option will appear when you have enabled the lab and clicked on **Save Changes**.

These are the options available:

- Compose
- Compose in a tab
- Search mail
- Back to threadlist
- Newer conversation
- Older conversation

- Select conversation
- Toggle star/Rotate among superstars
- Remove label
- Mute conversation
- Report as spam
- Delete
- Previous message
- Next message
- Reply
- Reply in a new window
- Reply all
- Reply all in a new window
- Forward
- Forward in a new window
- Search chat contacts
- Go to Inbox
- Go to Starred conversations
- Go to Sent messages
- Go to Drafts
- Go to All mail
- Go to Contacts
- Move focus to toolbar
- Select all conversations
- Deselect all conversations
- Select read conversations
- Select unread conversations
- Select starred conversations
- Select unstarred conversations
- Update conversation
- Remove label and go to previous conversation
- Remove label and go to next conversation
- Archive and go to previous conversation
- Archive and go to next conversation
- Undo last action
- Open "more actions" menu

18

- Mark as read
- Mark as unread
- Mark unread from the selected message
- Mark as not important
- Open keyboard shortcut help
- Archive
- Open "move to" menu
- Open "label as" menu
- Expand all
- Collapse all
- Open conversation
- Focus last mole
- Mark as important
- Go to next inbox section
- Go to previous inbox section
- Go to Label
- Go to Tasks
- Add conversation to Tasks
- Show menu
- Show Archived Hangouts
- Show Hangout requests
- Focus on the Conversation list
- Open phone

Google Calendar gadget

The Google calendar app will save you time by showing you your calendar events in the left column.

Mark as read button

This is an essential lab if you want to mark an email read and keep it in your inbox. It could also be used if you receive an email reply to another email which you were cc'd. You haven't read the original email as you saw the reply first. You read the reply but the original email is still unread in your inbox. Check the box next to it and click on the button **Mark as read** to solve this (or you could just open the email).

Multiple inboxes

This lab can keep your emails organized if you do not use the recommended Gmail inboxes. You can choose to have lists of email such as by label, archived or keyword. Once enabled go to the Multiple Inboxes in settings (**Gear wheel** > **Settings** > **Multiple Inboxes**) to set your preferences.

Some examples of new inboxes:

- Label:Shopping – This will show emails which have had the label Shopping applied to them. Substitute Shopping for one of your labels.
- is:unread – This will show only unread messages
- is:starred – This will show only starred messages
- is:sent – This will show emails that you've sent

Please note if you have enabled your inbox tabs, you must go to inbox in settings and uncheck all the inboxes you can, otherwise it will not work.

Warning, check to see if the settings button is on the top right of your screen when you enable Multiple inboxes. If it is no longer there, go back using your browser buttons and re-enable the Gmail inboxes. You don't want to be left without the ability to get to the settings options!

Preview pane

Do you miss the preview pane in Outlook and other traditional email programs? This lab allows you to get the familiar style inside Gmail. When you check a box in your list view you will be able to see the contents of the email in the new Preview Pane.

Once you have enabled the preview, you need to use the dropdown button on the top right of the screen and choose vertical or horizontal view as seen at the top of

18

the next figure. Grab the edge of the pane between the message list and the preview pane with your mouse to make it bigger or smaller.

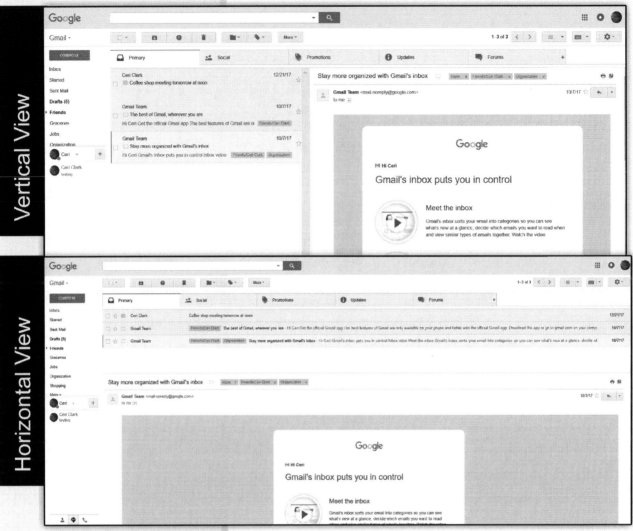

FIGURE 18.2 **Preview**
pane options

Right-side chat

As is suggested by the title you can move the chat from the left column to the right with this lab.

Smartlabels

This app automatically labels your emails based on what you've done before. Each time you open an email there will be a dropdown box where you can choose a category. After a while Gmail will learn what to label and you won't have to do it (much) anymore!

Unread Message Icon

Are you constantly flicking between tabs on your browser to see if you have any new emails? This lab can solve this problem but only if you use Chrome, Firefox or Opera. It will put a little unread message count number on the tab where you have your email open so you can just glance up rather than having to open the tab all the time.

FIGURE 18.3 Unread emails displayed in the browser tab.

Chapter summary

Labs extend the functionality of Gmail. There are plenty of functions that were labs in the past are now an integrated function of Gmail. For example you can now undo a sent email. In the last edition of this book, that lab appeared in this chapter. There are only ten labs now but they are worth looking at. They can change the way you work and make you more efficient while you are working. The labs discussed in this chapter are:

- Auto-advance
- Canned response
- Custom keyboard shortcuts
- Google Calendar gadget
- Mark as Read button
- Multiple inboxes
- Preview pane
- Right side chat
- Smartlabels
- Unread message icon

18

Frequently Asked Questions

What to expect in this chapter:

- How to get to Gmail

- Recovering or change a password

- Do you need a particular browser

- How to print emails from Gmail

- Using or removing the extra inboxes in Gmail

- How to remove people in a *Reply to all* before it is sent

- Increasing the size of the text in your browser

- Adding images to email

What is the address to login to Gmail?

http://mail.google.com or http://gmail.com

Help I've lost my password, what do I do now?

You've been on holiday or have had better things to do than check your email. You've opened up Gmail and you can't remember your password. Please use the following instructions to get your password sent to you:

1. Go to http://mail.google.com if you are not already on the login screen. Click on **Forgot password?** Click **Next**. If your password is correct you will be let in. If it isn't...
2. Click on **Try another way**
3. Choose to have Google send a verification code to the spare email address you nominated on your account. If it is correct you will be let in. If you don't have one...
4. Click on **Try another way**
5. Type in the phone number you nominated on your account. If it is correct you will be let in. If you didn't give a phone number...
6. Click on **Try another way**
7. Type in the month you created the account. If it is correct you will be asked to type in an email address you have access to...
8. Type in an email address, if Google doesn't recognise it, you will be refused access

Where do I go to change my password?

Go to **Settings** > **Account and Import** >

Change password.

Do I need a special browser to use Gmail?

Gmail runs on most browsers including Internet Explorer, Firefox, Chrome and Safari.

How do I print email?

This is easy. Enter the email you want to print. Look for the gray box on the top right of the email. Click on the arrow next to reply and select **Print**.

How do remove the 'extra' inboxes like updates, social and promotions?

Removing the extra inboxes can be done in two places. The easiest way to do this is to click on the plus sign at the end of the tabs row as seen circled in *figure 19.1*. You can also get to it by going to the **gear wheel** and choosing **Configure inbox**.

In the page that loads, uncheck all the tabs you can (you won't be able to get rid of the Primary inbox as it is the main one). Once you click **Save,** all your tabs will disappear leaving you with the one inbox.

The other way to turn off the other inboxes is to go to the **gear wheel** on the top right of your screen then **Settings > Inbox**.

In the **Categories** section, uncheck all the boxes bar Primary and then click on **Save Changes** at the bottom of the screen.

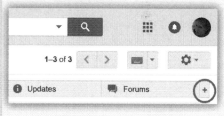

FIGURE 19.1 How to get to the inboxes screen.

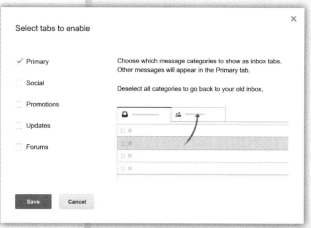

FIGURE 19.2 Uncheck the inboxes you don't want and click **Save**.

19

217

How do I remove email addresses when I Reply to All?

FIGURE 19.3 **Click on the x to remove an email address**

The way to remove email addresses when you reply to more than one person is to click on the email addresses to expand them and click on the x beside each address to remove them one-by-one.

How do I increase the size of the text in my browser and my Android phone?

To make anything bigger in Internet Explorer, you can change the text size by clicking on **View** in the top navigation bar and choosing **Text size**. You can change it in any browser by pressing down on the Ctrl key and then pushing away on your scroll wheel to make the page bigger or closer to you to make it smaller.

On your Android device you can make the text size bigger by changing them in your phone's main settings. These can be found at **Settings** > **Display** > **Font size** and you can also pinch and zoom inside emails.

If there are any questions you would like answered about Gmail that you think should be in this guide, visit http://www.CeriClark.com and have a look at my contact page. I will update the e-book with new additions to the FAQ.

How do I add images to my emails?

There are two ways to add images to an email. One way you can add them is by adding them as an attachment. Click on the paper clip as seen in figure 19.3, browse for the image on your computer and click open. The file may

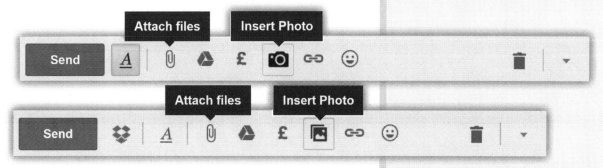

take a few seconds to load.

The second way to add an image is to click on the icon that looks like a couple of stacked pictures or the camera icon. It can appear as either in your Gmail account. Once clicked the instructions are the same as if you are adding a profile picture, please take a look at *Adding your profile picture* on page 30 for more detailed instructions on how to do this.

FIGURE 19.4 **Click on the paper clip to attach files, or the camera or picture icons to add pictur es inside the email.**

Chapter summary

This chapter covers questions that I have been asked, these are:

- What is the address to login to Gmail?
- Password change
- Help I've lost my password, what do I do now?
- Where do I go to change my password?
- Do I need a special browser to use Gmail?
- How do I print email?
- How do remove the 'extra' inboxes like updates, social and promotions?
- How do I remove email addresses when I Reply to All?
- How do I increase the size of the text in my browser and my Android phone?

19

Google Calendar

What to expect in this chapter:

- How to get to Google Calendar and a calendar overview

- Multiple calendars, the benefits and how to create, delete, use, edit and print them

- Changing the calendar view and appearance

- Sharing calendars including importing and exporting calendars

- What are flairs and how to use them

- How to set up and use goals, reminders and tasks in Google Calendar

FIGURE 20.1 Using the app launcher to get to Calendar.

Google's Calendar application is another service that is closely integrated with Gmail, as such this chapter will go into the basics and some tips that will show how Calendar can make your life easier.

How to get to Google Calendar

Google's Calendar service is available on your computer and your mobile device whether it is a phone or a tablet.

Getting to Calendar from your computer

Going directly there

Type in the following internet address in your browser to go directly there on your computer:

https://www.google.com/calendar

Click on **SIGN IN** on the top right of the screen. If you are logged in to any other Google service, you will not need to sign in again.

Navigate to Calendar from the app launcher

You can also get to Calendar using the App launcher. This is the button with nine squares located on the top right of your browser window when you are on any Google page. It is in the shape of a square as shown in *figure 20.1*. Click on the Calendar symbol and you will be taken to the service.

If you use Google Calendar a lot, you can move the Calendar icon in the app

FIGURE 20.2 Moving the Calendar icon in the App launcher.

launcher and move it to any location within it.

1. Ensure you are signed into any Google website
2. Click on the button with nine squares located on the top right of your browser window. This is also known as the App launcher button or a Waffle
3. Grab the Calendar icon with your mouse and drag it up to where you want it to be. In the example in *figure 20.2*, I have put it as the first icon but you can just as easily put it anywhere in the list

Google will remember this and it will appear at the top of every Google page where you are logged in.

Getting to Calendar from your mobile device

Google's Calendar app is available on Apple's iOS and Android's Gmail as well as on computers. Navigate to your mobile device's app store to download the app. Once you have done this, open up Calendar from your app list.

Calendar Overview

This section will give you an overview of the calendar homepage as illustrated in *figure 20.3* on the next page.

Toggle menu on and off

Remove or bring back the left hand menu by clicking on the three horizontal lines button.

Refresh events

If you cannot see any events you expect to see in your calendar or you are viewing somebody else's calendar, click on **Google Calendar** at the top of the page to refresh the events shown on the page.

Jump to today

Click on **Today** to jump to today from anywhere in the calendar.

Earlier or later time period

These arrows will let you move the main calendar view earlier or later. If you are viewing a week then you can go one week earlier or later, if you are viewing a month, it will go to the previous month or the next month and so on.

Search events

As with the Gmail website and emails, search your events by typing in this box. Advanced options are available by clicking on the arrow next to the box.

FIGURE 20.3 Calendar overview

Change view

View your Calendar with several different predefined views. These include:

- Day
- Week
- Month
- Year
- Schedule (Agenda)
- 4 days
- Show weekends
- Show declined events

These are the most popular ways to view your calendar but you can have custom views by highlighting a custom range on the month calendar in the menu on the left. This will be detailed more further in this chapter.

Settings

The gear wheel will take you to Calendar specific settings.

App launcher (other Google apps)

When you press on the squares (on the top right of your screen), you will be given the option to go to other Google services like Docs, Slides, Drive and Maps etc. You can add more apps to the initial list and re-arrange them as you prefer them laid out. For example, you may use Inbox and Docs more than any other Google service. The icons can be moved around so they appear at the top.

Notifications

These are Google+ and Google Photo notifications. You can safely ignore these if you have no intention of joining Google+ or using Google Photos.

Your account

Here you can change your account options, find out about Google's privacy policy and update your Google settings. This is where you can add or change your profile picture and manage your security settings for Google.

Left navigation menu

There are a few options in this navigation menu, here is a quick breakdown of what is possible from here.

Navigate and change view

Click and drag on any date to any other date and you will create a custom date view in the main window. This allows you to see a complete week at the end or the beginning of a month or a set number of days not catered to in the predefined view list.

Clicking on any date will bring up that date in the main calendar window.

Add calendars

This is where you can add a friend's calendar or click on the arrow to create new calendars. You can have multiple calendars for different areas of your personal and work life.

Show or hide calendars

In *My* or *Other calendars* you can check the boxes next to a calendar to show or hide events in the main calendar window. You can also remove calendars or change the color of calendar events by hovering over the calendar and clicking the three vertical dots for more settings.

Create an event

The red button with the plus button will allow you to

create new events in your calendar. Please note you can also create goals and reminders in your mobile phone app which will work nicely with the Inbox service. These will be discussed in detail further in this chapter.

Multiple Calendars

Google Calendar gives you the option of having many calendars. This is useful for having a personal or business calendar or you could have project calendars in a business scenario. Each member of your family could have their own calendar but you could view all the events as if they were in one calendar. The advantage of having multiple calendars is that you can turn off calendars temporarily to get a cleaner, uncluttered view if you need to. You could for example turn off your family calendars and just show the project you are working on during work hours. Google Calendar is very versatile.

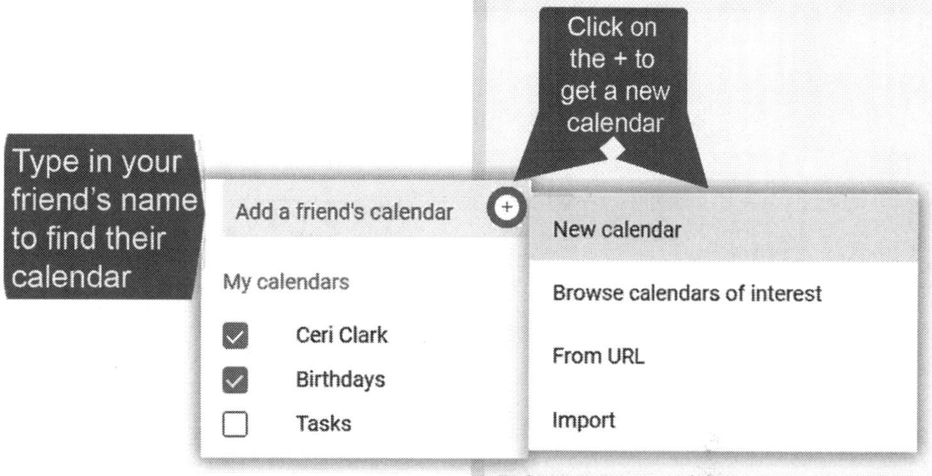

Type in your friend's name to find their calendar

Click on the + to get a new calendar

Add a friend's calendar   +

My calendars

☑ Ceri Clark

☑ Birthdays

☐ Tasks

New calendar

Browse calendars of interest

From URL

Import

FIGURE 20.4 Adding a calendar

Any tasks you make in Gmail will appear in your calendar when you check the box next to **Tasks** under your calendars in the left menu bar.

Adding calendars

As mentioned earlier you can create multiple calendars but you can also add other people's calendars. All the events will appear side by side in the main calendar window and you can show or hide events on a calendar basis.

Creating a new calendar

To create a new calendar that you own, click on the + next

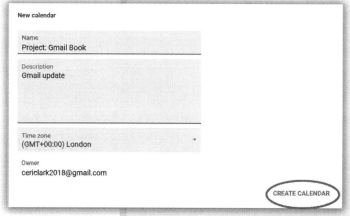

New calendar

Name
Project: Gmail Book

Description
Gmail update

Time zone
(GMT+00:00) London

Owner
cericlark2018@gmail.com

CREATE CALENDAR

FIGURE 20.5 Create a calendar pop-up.

20

to the box that says **Add a friend's calendar**. Select **New calendar** and a pop-up will load.

Type in your calendar's name, a description of the calendar and make sure that the time zone reflects the calendar's needs. If a project is done internationally but most of the participant's are in one country then it makes sense to make it the time zone of that country.

Click on **CREATE CALENDAR** and your calendar will be created.

To get back to the calendar homepage click on the arrow next to **Settings** at the top left of your screen.

You have a few seconds to click on **Configure** at the bottom of the screen. You will always be able to configure your calendar from the menu on the calendar homepage (hover over the calendar to get the menu button for the settings option) but if you want to get it right from the beginning then click on configure just after you've created it.

Configuring your calendar

You can get here by clicking on **Configure** that appears at the bottom of the screen after you have created the calendar or you can navigate to here by:

> **Calendar homepage > Hover over the calendar that you want to share > Menu button** (three vertical dots) > **Settings and Sharing**.

Please see the Settings section of this chapter for more information on how to configure your calendars.

Adding a friend's calendar

When you click into the box, a list will appear of some of your contacts. If the one you want is there, select that person, otherwise start typing their name and Google will suggest people from your contacts.

If you do not have permission to view your friend's/

FIGURE 20.6 Click into the box to start adding your friend's calendar.

family's/colleague's calendar, Google will ask if you want to send them a message to get permission.

Deleting calendars

Deleting a calendar is possible from the calendar settings and the calendar homepage. You cannot delete another person's calendar but you can unsubscribe from them. If you hover over the calendar you want to remove, click on the X that appears and it will be unsubscribed from. If it does not belong to you, the calendar can be brought back by clicking into the **Add a friend's calender** box and it will appear under **Other Calendars**.

There are some calendars that can be retrieved by clicking on **Settings** on the top right of the homepage and then finding the calendar on the left. Click on the crossed out eye to be able to see it again.

If you own the calendar you unsubscribe from, you cannot get it back.

Color-code calendars

When viewing your calendars, it is really helpful to color-code them so that you can see at a glance what events are due on a date or even over a month. You can color-code events but also calendars so that they have a certain color by default. This would be very helpful if you have personal and work calendars. You will be able to see immediately if you have a personal appointment during a work day. You would also be able to see at a glance what could possibly be rearranged.

Density and color

Head over to the gear wheel on the top right of your screen to choose **Density and color**. It should already be set to responsive which means it will pick the best 'look' for how big your screen is and the modern color scheme. Toggle between the options to find a combination you like.

20

Your default calendar

Your default calendar is the first calendar you have when you first open Google Calendar. It will have the name you opened up your Google account with. Events will be put in this calendar unless you choose another calendar. You can change the name and other settings on this calendar by hovering over it in the left hand menu and choosing the menu button (three vertical dots) and selecting **Settings and Sharing**.

Calendar appearance

There are several ways to view your calendars. You can zoom in to one day, a week, a month or zoom out to see a whole year.

Change the view

The options for viewing your calendar range from a day, week, year, your agenda (schedule) and 4 days. Click on any of these options to change how your calendar home page looks. Please see *figure 20.8* for how these look.

There is also a custom view where you can highlight a date range from the month view in the menu and the homepage will change to reflect this. If you want a three or six day view, or maybe you want to see what your appointments will be over the next two weeks. Click on the date and drag to the end date you want to see for a custom view. The new date range will appear on the homepage.

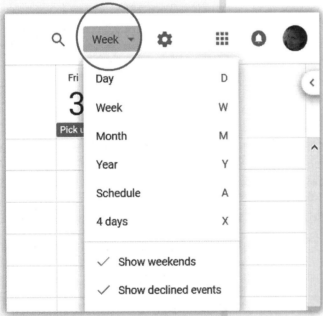

FIGURE 20.7 Choose a time period to view

Show or hide weekends

As in *figure 20.7*, click on the time period you want and select **Show weekends** to remove the tick. This will remove

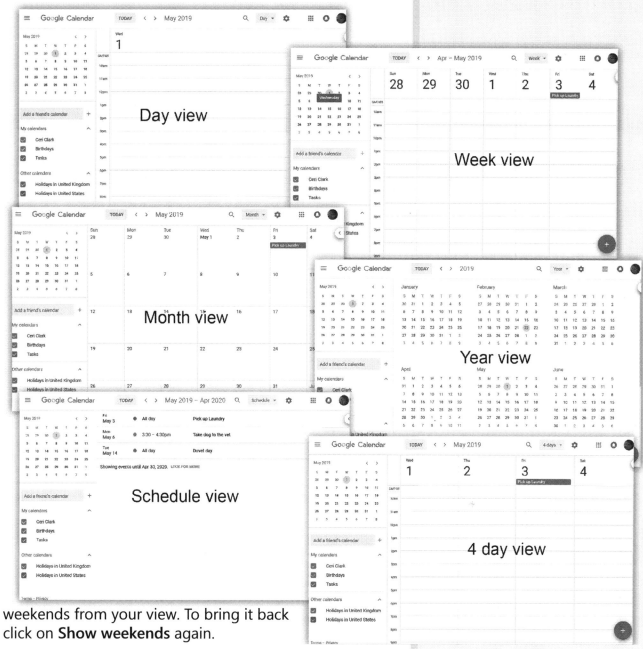

weekends from your view. To bring it back click on **Show weekends** again.

Show declined events

As illustrated in *figure 20.7*, at the bottom of the list, click on **show declined events** to remove the ticks and to remove declined events. Click on the option again to show them again.

FIGURE 20.8 How the different views look.

20

Create events

When you have your calendars all set up, it is time to add an event.

Using the + button

Click on the big red button with the plus on it at the bottom right of the screen.

The title (the Subject of your event)

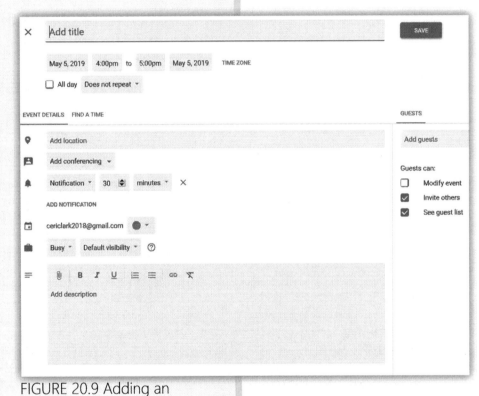

FIGURE 20.9 Adding an event.

In the pop-up type in your title. Be as descriptive as you can but as brief as you can. To help Google has created some flairs (background pictures) for certain events that are triggered by keywords. I will go into more depth with these in the Flairs section. For example Dinner with James Smith.

Date

Next, click into the date and choose the date you need from the dropdown calendar (month view).

Time

Next to the date, choose the start time and the end time. Notice the Time Zone next to the times? Click on this and it gives you the option of having a separate time zone for the beginning and end of your event. This is particularly useful if you are taking a flight and you are leaving in one time zone but arriving in another!

Location

You can put a location next. It accepts zip/postal codes and you will be able to click on it and go to Google Maps if you do this. However, if you don't need the location on your calendar (you can still put it in the description) then you can have a flair as your background picture if you have one. If Google has a picture of your location on Google Maps it will put the image into your event after it is submitted to make it easier to see. At the time of writing these pictures appeared when you click on an event in a browser on your computer but they appear in your event list on a mobile device. If you want to use background pictures, your decision on what you want to use will be determined by how you view your calendar.

Add conferencing

Add a Google Hangout to your invitation by choosing this option from the drop-down list.

Notifications

Choose whether you want a notification or an email before the event. You can have several of these. You can have an email at the beginning of the week to remind yourself that there will be an event. Another one on the day and a notification just before the event in case you get distracted.

Which calendar?

If you have more than one calendar, you can choose which one to put your event in. This is useful if you have shared your calendars with certain groups so they will be automatically updated with your event without having to send an invitation. If there are changes to your events, check the calendar before you go to it in case the date, time or location has changed. Even if you have not been

Please be aware that if you have already accepted an invitation to an event, the date, time and location may change without you being notified.

Your event will be updated automatically in your calendar but you will not be emailed or otherwise notified unless an update is specifically sent.

This is also true if your attendees use a different calendar such as Outlook for example. They will be notified by email and they will have to load a file into their calendar application to get the updated information.

If you want your attendees to know of changes you make to your events, make sure you click send updates when you save the changes.

sent an update, changes will be reflected in your calendar. This is unique to Google Calendar as other calendar applications require you to be sent updates for changes to be applied to attendee calendars.

Busy?

If you say you are busy, then it will show up when someone else is trying to schedule you.

Description

Put as much or as little information as you want in here. Bear in mind that others may be reading the description so you may or may not want to put personal information in your descriptions.

Inviting guests

Inviting guests is an important feature of Google Calendar. You can give them permissions to change the event and you can even find mutual agreeable times for meetings.

Optional attendance

When you hover over your guest's name on the right of the page you will see a little icon of a person. Click on that and you can choose to make that person's attendance optional. Click on the icon again to make their presence a requirement.

Guest permissions

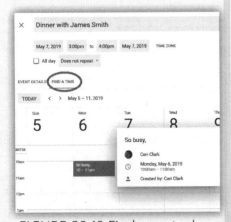

FIGURE 20.10 Find a mutual agreeable time for your meeting using **FIND A TIME**.

When you invite someone to your event, it appears in their calendar. You can choose whether they are allowed to modify the event, invite others or see the guest list. This only applies to other Google users. If they are outside the Google system they will have to download an iCal file and load it into their calendar manually.

Find time (scheduling event times to suit everyone)

Under the time and date information beside the **EVENT DETAILS** you will find **FIND A TIME**. Click on this and you will be able to see when your guests are available. Of course this only works if your invited attendees are Google Calendar users themselves.

On the right you can add guests and toggle their calendars on and off. Choose a date and time where you are all free.

When all the details are filled in to your satisfaction click on **SAVE** at the top of your screen by the title of the event and your event will not only be created but invites will be sent to your guests.

By typing into the Calendar

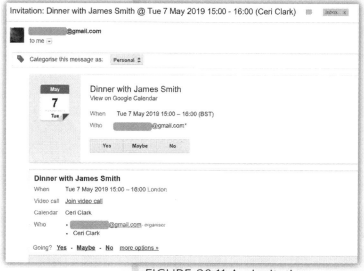

FIGURE 20.11 An invitation sent by email.

Click into a date in your calendar and type as if you were talking to a personal assistant, for example, **Dinner with Dave**. Click into the dates and times to change them. You can edit the event by finding it on the date and clicking on the entry and then the edit button (pencil in circle).

Responding to an event

If you have been sent an invitation by email, select your response from the buttons presented in the email. The options are **Yes**, **Maybe** and **No**. The button will change color but nothing will happen but it will show you are going within the event in the calendar.

You can also accept an invitation from the calendar entry itself.

FIGURE 20.12 Example event card.

Click on the entry in your calendar homepage and you will

see at the bottom of the pop up '**Going?**' On the right next to this it will say **YES, NO** and **MAYBE**. Choose the option that suits your schedule.

You can see who else is going if you are the organiser or if your organiser has allowed you to, as can be see in *figure 20.12*.

If the attendee does not respond they will show up as not responding in Google Calendar.

Please be aware that these steps may not apply to your attendees who are outside of the Google system and use different Calendar applications. They will get the email but they may not be able to accept the invitation because they don't have a Google account that will allow them to do so. They will have an ICS file which they will put into their own Calendar system but it may be completely separate. Any changes you make will have to be sent to them as an update so they can manually add the file to reflect changes to their calendar. However, if they are in the Google system, it will happen automatically.

Flairs

Flairs are pictures that Google has created to illustrate Calendar entries. A typical example can be seen in *figure 20.12*. Typing in certain keywords will bring up pictures. There is no definitive list of these flairs as more are added all the time and some maybe taken away but here is a list compiled from forums on the internet on what has worked for many people. Some flairs will only work for certain countries and there may be more that have not been found (as there are lists for different countries).

All the images belong to Google and are copyrighted so shouldn't be used outside of Google Calendar. They are shown in this book for educational use.

The words in bold below are categories within the larger categories I have listed. The keywords after the colon are the flair names. These were tested at the time of writing and appear as images in the figures on these pages.

236

Communication and Media

book club: book club

cinema: cinema, movies

communication: reach out to, write letter, send invitations

reading: reading, newspaper, ebook

Education and Learning

computer science: learn to code, coding time, hackathon, Rails Girls, Railsgirls, Hour of Code, Codecademy, Computer Science, Programming in Python, Programming in Java, Web Development, Web Programming

graduation: graduation

languages: Arabic Class, Arabic Course, Bulgarian Class, Bulgarian Course, Catalan Class, Catalan Course, Chinese Class, Chinese Course, Croatian Class, Croatian Course,Czech Class, Czech Course, Danish Class, Danish Course, Dutch Class, Dutch Course, English Class, English Course, Farsi Class, Farsi Course, Filipino Class, Filipino Course, Finnish Class, Finnish Course, French Class, French Course, German Class, German Course, Greek Class, Greek Course, Hebrew Class, Hebrew Course, Hindi Class, Hindi Course, Hungarian Class, Hungarian Course, Indonesian Class, Indonesian Course, Italian Class, Italian Course, Japanese Class, Japanese Course, Korean Class, Korean Course, Latvian Class, Latvian Course, Lithuanian Class, Lithuanian Course, Norwegian Class, Norwegian Course, Polish Class, Polish Course, Portuguese Class, Portuguese Course, Practice Arabic, Practice Bulgarian, Practice Catalan, Practice Chinese, Practice Croatian, Practice Czech, Practice Danish, Practice Dutch, Practice English, Practice Farsi, Practice Filipino, Practice Finnish, Practice French, Practice German, Practice Greek, Practice Hebrew, Practice Hindi, Practice Hungarian,

FIGURE 20.13 Communication and media flairs.

FIGURE 20.14 Education and Learning.

Practice Indonesian, Practice Italian, Practice Japanese, Practice Korean, Practice Latvian, Practice Lithuanian, Practice Norwegian, Practice Polish, Practice Portuguese, Practice Russian, Practice Slovak, Practice Slovenian, Practice Spanish, Practice Swedish, Practice Thai, Practice Turkish, Practice Ukranian, Practice Vietnamese, Russian Class, RussianCourse, Slovak Class, Slovak Course, Slovenian Class, Slovenian Course, Spanish Class, Spanish Course, Swedish Class, Swedish Course, Thai Class, Thai Course, Turkish Class, Turkish Course, Ukranian Class, Ukranian Course, Vietnamese Class, Vietnamese Course

music class: piano, singing, music class, choir practice, flute, orchestra, oboe, clarinet, saxophone, cornett, trumpet, contrabass, cello, trombone, tuba, music ensemble, string quartett, guitar lesson, classical music, choir

Food and Drink

FIGURE 20.15 Food and Drink flairs.

bbq: bbq, barbecue, barbeque

beer: beer, beers, Oktoberfest, October Fest, Octoberfest

breakfast: breakfast, breakfasts, brunch, brunches

coffee: coffee, coffees

cooking: cooking

dinner: dinner, dinners, restaurant, restaurants, Family meal

drinks: cocktail, drinks, cocktails

lunch: lunch, lunches, luncheon

Health and Grooming

dentist: dentist, dentistry, dental

haircut: haircut, hair

manicure: manicure, pedicure, manicures, pedicures

massage: massage, back rub, backrub, massages

Hobbies, Leisure and Sport

american football: football

art: painting, art workshop, art workshops, sketching workshop, drawing workshop

badminton: badminton

baseball: baseball

basketball: basketball

billiard: billiard

bookclub: book club, reading

bowling: bowling

boxing: boxing

cinema: cinema, movies

cycling: bicycle, cycling, bike, bicycles, bikes, biking

dancing: dance, dancing, dances

golf: golf

gym: gym, workout, workouts

hiking: hiking, hike, hikes

kayaking: kayaking

pingpong: ping pong, table tennis, ping-pong, pingpong

running: jog, jogging, running, jogs, runs

sailing: sail, sailing, boat cruise, sailboat

skiing: skiing, ski, skis, Snowboarding, snowshoeing, snow shoe, snow boarding

soccer: soccer

swimming: swim, swimming, swims tennis: tennis

walk: going for a walk, walking

yoga: yoga

Holidays and Travel

camping: camping

chinesenewyear: chinese new year, chinese new years, chinese new year's

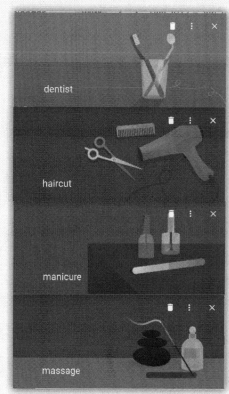

FIGURE 20.16 Health and Grooming flairs.

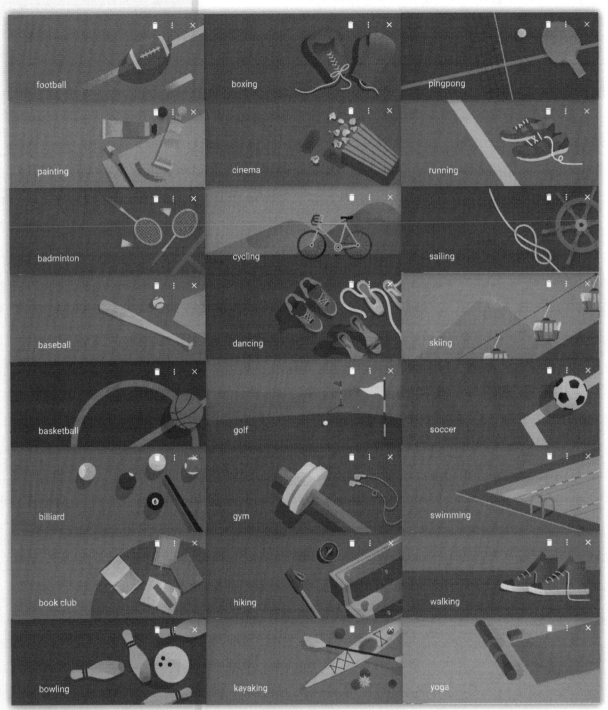

FIGURE 20.17 Hobbies, leisure and sport flairs.

halloween: halloween, helloween, hallowe'en, Allhalloween, All Hallows' Eve, All Saints' Eve

newyear: new year, new year's, new years

santa: Santa Claus, Father Christmas

thanksgiving: thanksgiving

xmas: christmas, xmas, x-mas, boxing day

xmas meal: christmas dinner, christmas lunch, christmas brunch, christmas luncheon, xmas lunch, xmas luncheon, x-mas dinner, x-mas lunch, x-mas brunch, x-mas luncheon, christmas eve dinner, christmas eve lunch, christmas eve brunch, christmas eve luncheon, xmas eve dinner, xmas eve lunch, xmas eve brunch, xmas eve luncheon, x-mas eve dinner, x-mas eve lunch, x-mas eve brunch, x-mas eve luncheon

xmas party: christmas party, xmas party, x-mas party, christmas eve party, xmas eve party, x-mas eve party

Household

clean: cleaning, clean the house, clean the apartment, clean house, tidy up, vacuum clean, vacuum cleaning

oilchange: oil change, car service

repair: fridge repair, handyman, electrician, DIY, electrician

LGBTQ

pride: christopher street day, dyke march, gay parade, gay pride, gayglers, gaygler, lesbian march, lesbian parade, lesbian pride, euro pride, europride, world pride, worldpride

Life Events

graduation: graduation

wedding: wedding, wedding eve, wedding-eve party, weddings

FIGURE 20.18 Holiday flairs

20

world pride

graduation

wedding

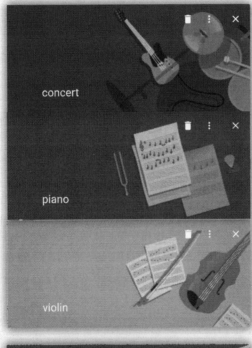

concert

piano

violin

plan week

Music

concert: concert, gig, concerts, gigs

instruments: piano, string quartett, singing, saxophone, orchestra, oboe, music ensemble, music class, tuba, trumpet, trombone, guitar lesson, flute, cornett, contrabass, classical music, clarinet, choir practice, choir, cello

violin: violin, violins

Planning

plan my day: plan week, plan quarter, plan day, plan vacation, week planning, vacation planning

One flair can be used to illustrate many activities and even though you may have chosen a keyword to make one appear, if you have set a location for your event and Google has an image for that place, it will supersede the flair keywords.

Delete and get your events back

If you want to delete your calendar events, click on your event and then click on the trash can (bin) symbol that appears at the top of your pop up. In your Google Calendar app, you need to press on the menu button on the top right of the event to delete it.

If you want to delete **all** events in your trash, on your computer, at the top right, click **Empty trash/bin**.

You can restore deleted event entries up to 30 days after you removed it. In Calendar, go to the **Gear wheel** at the top of the screen and press on **Trash** in the US or **Bin** in the UK. On the far right of your event entry you can restore it (arrow pointing left) or delete it forever (trash/bin symbol).

Settings

There are two ways to get to the settings:

From the top of the screen, click on the **Gear wheel** and choose **Settings**. The other way is to click on the menu button from the calendars in the left menu, please follow these steps:

1. Hover over the calendar you want to share and click on the menu button (three vertical dots)
2. Choose **Settings and sharing**

The method of getting to Settings will determine where in your settings the page will load.

On the left you will see **General**. These are the options that will appear if you go to the top of the page and select the **gear wheel** and then **Settings**.

General Settings

You can scroll down the main window to get to any of these sections or click on the headings in the left menu. You can collapse the general settings in the left menu by clicking on the arrow next to **General** in the menu.

Language and region Select your region to get the correct language. In the US, deleted items will be in the trash and in the UK it will go in the bin, etc.

Time zone You can set a secondary time zone here. More information is in the Time zone section of this chapter.

Did you know...

You can add an iCal Calendar to your Google Calendar and it will continually update without you doing anything.

If you are using Microsoft Outlook, you can add an iCal Calendar as an internet calendar and it will update your Calendar with details as they change. What is really happening with Outlook is that it is looking at the internet periodically and downloading (and loading) the file so you don't have to.

Did you know...

An iCal Calendar uses an ics file. When you export an iCal Calendar you will get an ics file to add to your calendar.

World clock Show more than one clock across the world.

Event settings When you create an event, calendar will suggest time periods. You can also always set the guest permissions so that you don't have to set it a particular way each time you make an event.

View options If you only use this as a work calendar and you only work week days, you can set the Calendar so it only shows the week days. Other options include; show declined events, reduce the brightness of past events, view calendars side by side in Day View, start the week, on Saturday, Sunday or Monday, what time period you want to see when you load Calendar and if you want an alternate calendar, in a different language.

Events from Gmail Add events automatically from Gmail.

Keyboard shortcuts Check the box if you want to be able to use keyboard shortcuts.

In the left menu under General you will see **Add Calendar**.

Add Calendar options

New Calendar Create a new calendar from here.

Browse Calendars of Interest Browse calendars that are already set up which include holidays, sports, phases of the moon and a calendar that contains week numbers.

From URL If you have the URL of an iCal Calendar, this is where you add it.

Import & export

Please see *Importing and exporting your calendars* later in this chapter.

Calendar specific options

Calendar Settings These are what you initially set in the calendar information, (name, description and time zone).

Auto-accept invitations Do you want to allow people send you invitations which automatically appear in your calendar?

Access permissions Here you set the calendar to be seen by the public. You also can set it so that they see the detail or only if it is free or busy.

Share with specific people You can let only certain people see your calendar.

Event notifications This is your default notification for all events on the Calendar you are configuring. How soon before your event do you want to be notified? Would you like it to be a notification or an email?

All-day event notifications Choose the way you want to be notified of all day events here.

General notifications How do you want to be notified for new events? This could be when someone sends you an invitation or when they change, cancel, respond, (where guests respond to an event for which you can see the guest list and your daily agenda), or receive an email with your agenda (every day at 5am in your current time zone).

Integrate calendar This is where you get the code to share the calendar or embed it in to a website.

Remove calendar Here you can unsubscribe from a calendar or delete it entirely.

Under the gear wheel there are a few extra settings which are:

- **Trash** Go here to see events that you have deleted to either remove them completely or restore them.

- **Density and color** Choose whether you want the calendar to respond to the size of the window or be compact and if you want modern or classic colors.

- **Print** Print out the calendar you are viewing from

FIGURE 20.23 How to get to your Calendar's settings.

here. Please take a look at Printing your calendar for more information on this.

- **Back to Classic Calendar** (this may be taken away at some point).
- **Send Feedback** Let Google know if you love or hate features and even suggest new ones.
- **Help** Take a look at Google's own help pages.

Embedding your Calendar in a website

Embed your calendar is a feature for your websites. Embed the code to let people know events. These events will be public and would be useful if you want to let people know where you are if you are a musician, author or someone who sells craft items at fairs. This could be an elegant solution for letting people know what you are doing in your professional life.

1. Hover over the calendar you want to share and click on the menu button (three vertical dots).
2. Choose **Settings and sharing**.
3. Either click on **Integrate calendar** in the left menu or scroll down to the section.
4. Click on the code under **Embed code** and right-click to copy it.
5. Embed it in the code of your website.

Time zones

If you are traveling to a different time zone, you can get Calendar to set a beginning and end time in different time zones. If you work with anyone in another time zone or don't want to wake up a friend or a family member in a different country by accident, knowing the local time is a must. Get Google Calendar to show you the other time zones to avoid any mishaps.

To get to the time zone options:

1. Click on the **gear wheel** on the top right of the screen
2. Click on **Settings**

Google will show you your local time zone in Calendar so it is important to set the correct time but it will also show you the local time when you are travelling to another time zone.

The first 3 'cards' in **Settings** are **Language and region**, **Time zone** and **World clock**. Make sure all these cards are set to get the benefit of the time zone options.

Sharing Calendars

Sharing your calendar will help your friends, family or co-workers to organize your events. They will not only see when you are available but they will be able to use the scheduling option in Google to create events that will suit everyone who needs to go.

Sharing your calendar by invitation

You can share your calendar by inviting people in the settings.

1. In the left navigation menu, hover over the calendar you want to share and click on the menu button (three vertical dots)
2. Click on Settings and sharing
3. Scroll down to share with specific people.
4. Click on **ADD PEOPLE**
5. Add an email address or start typing a contact's name and choose their name when you see it
6. Decide which permission you want your invitee to have
7. Click **SEND**

Your contact will get an email and they can choose to add your calendar to their calendar by searching for your name in the **Add a friend's calendar/Add a co-worker's** section of Google Calendar.

FIGURE 20.24 Find the Import option by clicking on the plus next to **Add a friend's calendar**.

Importing and exporting calendars

Add or export calendar or event information using the import and export options in Google Calendar. This section covers the option for adding a friend's calendar or sharing your calendars with them.

Importing

Reasons for importing a calendar could be to move from a different calendar application or to see someone else's events in a file that they have given you. These are the steps to import a calendar from a file into Google Calendar.

1. In the left menu, look for **Add a friend's calendar**. It may say add a co-worker's calendar if you have access to the paid version. Click on the plus next to this

2. Choose Import from the menu that loads as illustrated in figure 20.24

3. Browse your computer for the file you want to import and click **Open**

4. Click on **Import**

The events will appear in your calendar. You can also get to **Import** from the settings under the gear wheel. It will be at the top left of the settings page when you click on **Import & export**.

Exporting

Your reasons for exporting your calendars could be to share your calendar with other people but you might also want to download and keep the ICS file for back up purposes.

1. Go to the **gear wheel** on the top right of Google Calendar

2. Choose **Settings**

3. Select **Import & export**

4. Choose **EXPORT**. All your calendars will be exported in a single Zip file

5. Choose where you want the file to be saved on your computer and click **Save**. You can rename it to make it easier to find if you wish

6. Unzip the file (in windows right-click and choose **Extract All**)

7. Each calendar will be in a different file with an ICS ending. Choose which calendars/files you want to share or backup and download the file

Keyboard shortcuts

To turn this option on, scroll down to the bottom of the **Settings** page and check the box next to Keyboard shortcuts.:

1. Click on the Gear wheel on the top right of the screen

2. Click on **Settings**

Printing your calendar

When you print your calendar, it will print the view that you are seeing. If you are viewing the monthly view then you will get a grid but if you are viewing the schedule, you

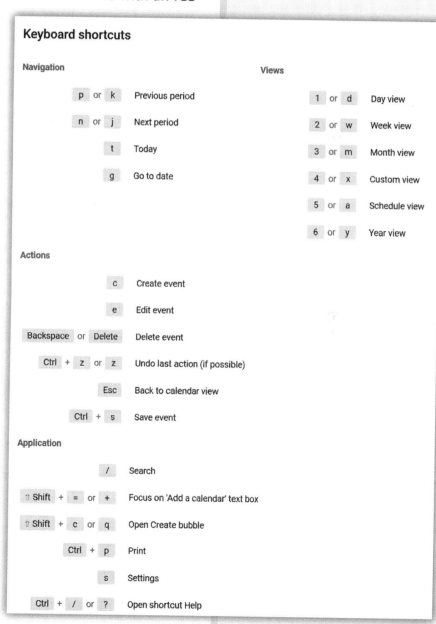

Keyboard shortcuts

Navigation

p or k	Previous period
n or j	Next period
t	Today
g	Go to date

Views

1 or d	Day view
2 or w	Week view
3 or m	Month view
4 or x	Custom view
5 or a	Schedule view
6 or y	Year view

Actions

c	Create event
e	Edit event
Backspace or Delete	Delete event
Ctrl + z or z	Undo last action (if possible)
Esc	Back to calendar view
Ctrl + s	Save event

Application

/	Search
⇧ Shift + = or +	Focus on 'Add a calendar' text box
⇧ Shift + c or q	Open Create bubble
Ctrl + p	Print
s	Settings
Ctrl + / or ?	Open shortcut Help

FIGURE 20.25 Keyboard shortcuts.

20

will get a list of your appointments in the coming days.

1. Click on the **Gear wheel** on the top right of the screen.
2. Click on **Print**.

On the pop-up you can choose what range of dates you want to print. There is a choice of font sizes ranging from smallest to biggest (this will change the number of pages you will have to print).

Other options are:

- Portrait or landscape
- Show events that you've declined
- Black and white
- More options
- Print descriptions
- Print end times
- Print your response

Click **PRINT** to send it to your printer.

Goals (Only on your mobile device)

When you use the Google Calendar app on your mobile device you can choose to set goals. This could be a gym visit. If you feel you can't do the gym visit, Calendar will reschedule for a more suitable time.

1. On your Calendar app, press the red circle with the plus sign in it
2. Choose Goal
3. Select from the list: Exercise, Build a skill, Family & friends, Me time and Organise my life
4. Narrow down your option
5. How often?
6. For how long?
7. Best time? Morning, afternoon, evening or anytime

8. For most skills, Calendar will schedule a time, but for exercise, connect to Google Fit

When all the steps are done Calendar will suggest a time, you can readjust this to a different time but you don't have control over the time. It will search your Calendar for free times. You can however snooze the events if you are not ready on a particular day.

One more word of warning. You cannot choose a start date. Be ready to do the goal you are setting as Calendar will schedule the first 'event' for tomorrow!

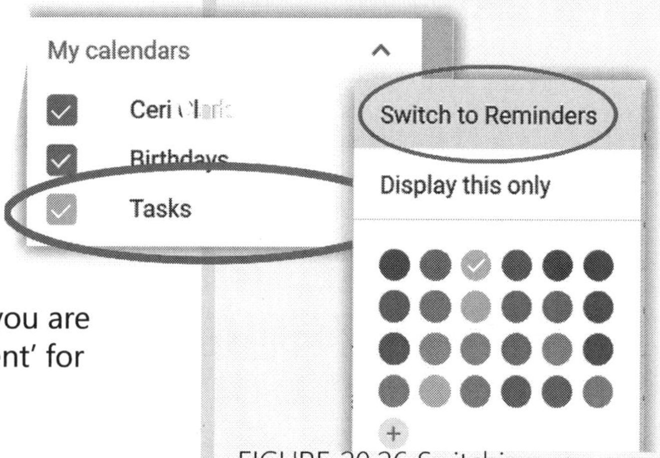

Reminders

Reminders can be viewed and made in Calendar as well as Inbox by Gmail. If you can't see reminders in the left menu in Calendar, then click on the arrow to the right of Tasks and choose **Switch to Reminders**.

Create a Reminder

Reminders can be viewed and created in Google Keep, Inbox by Gmail and Google Calendar. These are the steps for creating them in Google Calendar:

1. Click into a date (or time frame if you are in day mode)
2. Choose **Reminder**. It will go blue when it is selected
3. Alter the time and dates if necessary and choose whether you want the reminder to repeat
4. Click on SAVE

At the time of writing, flairs did not work with Reminders.

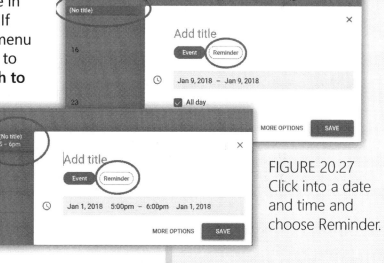

FIGURE 20.26 Switching Tasks to Reminders

FIGURE 20.27 Click into a date and time and choose Reminder.

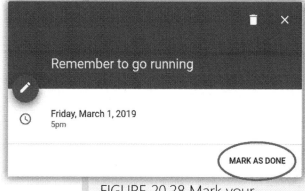

FIGURE 20.28 Mark your Reminder as done.

20

If you want to edit your reminder, click on it and choose the pencil symbol that appears on the card.

Remove reminders

Find the reminder you want to remove, select it and choose **Mark as Done**.

Tasks

Tasks are available in Google Calendar. If you cannot see it in the left navigation menu, click on the arrow next to **Reminders** in your **My Calendars** section and choose **Switch to Tasks**.

Viewing Tasks

Click into the box next to **Tasks** to view them in a list on the right of the Calendar screen. If you cannot see it, there is a tab with an arrow in it that you can click on to make the list visible. To collapse the list, click on the arrow again as shown in *figure 20.30*.

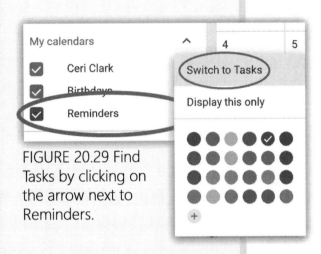

FIGURE 20.29 Find Tasks by clicking on the arrow next to Reminders.

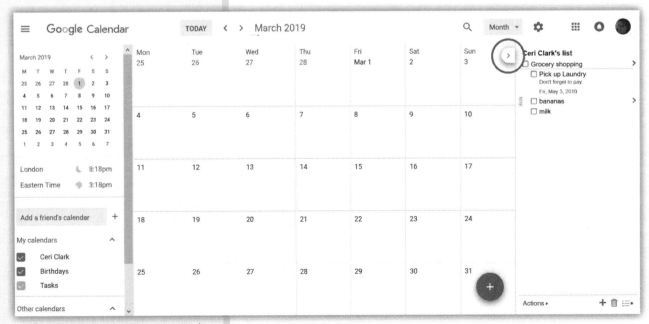

FIGURE 20.30 Viewing Tasks in Google Calendar.

Creating, editing and deleting tasks is the same as if you are in Gmail. Please see *Chapter 14 Tasks* for more information on how to do these.

Chapter summary

With a mix of events, reminders, tasks and goals, Google Calendar aims to supercharge the way you organize your time. This chapter gives you an overview of what is possible and how to achieve certain functions within the service. Google Calendar integrates with Gmail which gives it a place in this book.

The beginning of this chapter covered how to get to Google Calendar using the address bar and the app launcher which appears in ever Google service where you are signed in.

Next was a calendar overview which covered the main features from the calendar homepage and how to navigate it.

Multiple calendars are an essential feature of Google Calendar, allowing you to separate your life into calendars so that you can turn events on and off by category. Turn off your personal calendar to concentrate on your work appointments for example.

Adding calendars, configuring them and your default calendar are all detailed next along with how to add a friend's calendar. Color coding your calendars allow you to see at a glance what you have planned for the day, week or month. Choosing a density and color will personalize your calendar even further.

Changing the view of your calendar can help you to focus on what needs to be done. Only looking at what needs to be done a day or a week can affect how you work. Taking a macro or micro view of your life can help you to plan how to want to spend your time. The calendar appearance section details how to show or hide weekends and show declined events

A chapter on Google Calendar wouldn't be complete without a section on creating events and of course responding to them once you have been extended an invitation.

Flairs are pictures that Google have created to illustrate certain events. Typing keywords into your event title will make these pictures appear. In the flairs section of this chapter, there is an index of the keywords and images that go with each keyword. Drill down the categories to find the keyword that best illustrates your event and it will show when you click on your event and on your calendar entries on your mobile device.

Another section discusses deleting events and how to get them back.

There are two ways to get to the settings in Google Calendar. The settings section gives you an overview of what is available and how to use them.

If you would like your calendar to be public there is no better way than to embed your calendar into your website. Take a look at **Embedding your Calendar** in a website for more information on how to do this.

The next section goes into how to individualise Google Calendar for your time zone and how to view different time zones within Google Calendar. Features include how to set a beginning and end time to an event which start and finish in different time zones as well as seeing different time zones from within the left menu.

Sharing calendars through inviting people and also Importing and exporting calendars are shown and the keyboard shortcuts available for Google Calendar are detailed. The gear wheel is where you go to print your calendar.

Another feature which hooks in Gmail and Inbox by Gmail is goal setting, reminders and tasks. The last few sections in this chapter discuss how to create and remove reminders and how you can use tasks in Calendar.

Glossary

	2-step verification	A security feature where two items are needed to log in to a website. This is usually a password and some other form of identification such as a code from a mobile device.
A	**Address bar**	The box at the top of your browser where website addresses show, for example http://gmail.com
	Address book	Similar to an old-style book where addresses were written in a book but held electronically in Gmail.
	Adobe Flash	This is software which operates in browsers that is created by Adobe to view interactive elements on a webpage.
	Android device	These are smartphones and tablets which run on Google's operating system, Android.
	App	Short for application, these are small programs which run on mobile devices such as smartphones and tablets
	Archive	Archiving emails means in the strictest sense that the label inbox has been removed from an email and is no longer in your inbox. You can find any email in All Mail unless it has been deleted.
	Attachment	This is a document, picture or anything that can be 'attached' to an email.
B	**Browser**	This is a computer program that allows you to view webpages.
C	**Captcha**	Also known as word verification, this box, usually containing letters or numbers is used to prove that people submitting to a website are not robots. Captcha can also be images.
	Chat	In Gmail, this can be talking using text or your webcam.
	Contacts	People you have connected with by Gmail or Google+.

Text file which contains simple information such as exported contact information. This type of document can be opened in text or spreadsheet applications.

CSV

A number of emails grouped together with a common subject.

Discussion thread

Google's free online storage of files and photos. It is also the place where you can create free spreadsheets and documents.

Drive

D

This is a feature where you can download some data or a document that can be saved on your computer which can then be used on a different account or application.

Export

E

An application on your computer which allows you to find files, folder, and software on your PC. This is called Finder on Macs.

File Explorer

F

A feature of Gmail that sorts your email by predetermined elements. This can be for example filtering your email so all emails from a certain address will go into a finance folder (label).

Filters

The symbol located on the top right of Google pages that will take you to the settings for that service.

Gear wheel

G

A unit of computer storage. At the time of writing Google gives you 15 Gigabytes of space. This is roughly equivalent to 200,000 emails.

Gigabytes

The free email service provided by Google.

Gmail

There are good or bad hackers but for the purposes of this book, I refer to those nefarious people who have devoted their lives to harming you or others by breaking in to computers and websites.

Hackers

H

Hangouts refer to connecting to people by both instant messaging (text chat) and video chats with webcams.

Hangouts

Hashtags	These are words preceded by the # symbol. For example #cooking is a hashtag.
Homepage	The start page of a website, also known as the main page.
I **Icon**	A picture or symbol which when pressed takes you to another webpage or function (such as a Google Hangout).
Images	Photos, pictures and graphics.
Import	This is a feature where you can upload some data or a document to a web service like Gmail or Google+.
Inbox	This is an electronic folder which holds your emails. Traditionally your inbox was one folder where all your emails first arrived. Gmail now provides several inboxes which sort your emails into categories.
K **Kindle**	This is a device which uses the AZW or Mobi e-book formats.
L **Labs**	Google Labs are experimental features that Google are testing. They may disappear at any time or if they become popular, appear as standard options later.
Labels	Labels are what folders are in other programs. You assign a label to an email to sort them. Click on a label to find other emails of the same type.
Lastpass	This is a service from lastpass.com where you can store all your passwords in the cloud which is protected by one password and 2-factor authentication for extra security. Use this service to generate a different password for every website you sign up to but you will only have to remember the one.
N **Nested label**	A nested label means that a label will appear under another in the label list.

A string of letters and numbers which can be a phrase or random which allows you access to a website or service.	**Password**
A computer that runs the Windows operating system.	**PC**
This is where criminals will try to get your personal information from you by sending emails that appear to be from people or organizations you trust. This can be usernames, passwords and/or credit card information.	**Phishing**
In the context of this book this is your information held by Google.	**Profile**
Schemes designed to commit fraud.	**Scams**
Text that finishes off an email. This is usually your name but can include your address, email address, phone numbers and images.	**Signature**
Irrelevant, unwanted and unasked-for emails.	**Spam**
The subject of your email should be a short description of the contents of the email.	**Subject**
See 2-step verification	**Two-factor authentication**
URL is short for Uniform Resource Locator. It is a quick way of saying web address.	**URL**
Get rid of emails you no longer want by following the instructions at the bottom of emails to unsubscribe from future messages.	**Unsubscribe**
A unique piece of information used as a means to identify you to Google.	**Username**
This is a way of sending contact information in the form of a document. Import vCards to Gmail to fill in details of a contact.	**vCard**

P

S

T
U

V

W

Webcam

Webcam A video camera which will enable you to talk face-to-face in Google Hangouts.

Word verification

See Captcha

Index

T

U

W

About Ceri Clark

Ceri Clark is a full-time author and mother. She was a Librarian with over eleven years of experience in corporate, public and private libraries culminating in a Library Manager position at the ill-fated English Audit Commission.

Following the closure of the library (and the future demise of the organization) she began to utilize her skills for searching, writing and advising with her Simpler Guides Series. Find out more about Ceri Clark at cericlark.com.

DISGUISED PASSWORD BOOKS
A safer way to write your passwords down

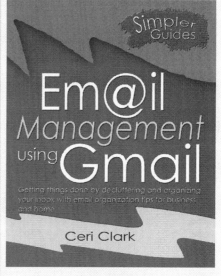

Simpler Guides

81524196R00151

Made in the USA
San Bernardino, CA
08 July 2018